The Path of Power and Wisdom

The magic of strategy isn't limited to armies and politicians. This book makes it easy to use strategy in every facet of your life. The way of the warrior is a special path. Warriors control their destinies while regular people accept their fate. Though everyone uses the word "strategy," only skilled warriors know its secret principles. Strategy isn't a plan, and having a strategy isn't like having a good idea. Strategy is a process and a way of seeing the world.

For over 2,500 years, Sun Tzu's *The Art of War* has been used to train warriors in the magic of strategy. For most of that history, however, rulers kept regular people from learning its secrets. Not only was the text kept from the masses, but the book itself was written in a subtle code. For the unintiated who don't understand that code, the book is only half complete, designed to be confusing and contradictory.

The Warrior's Apprentice unlocks the secrets of *The Art of War* so that anyone can master the skills of the warrior. It completes the original, putting its lessons into an easy-to-use form. The simplest way to use this work is to read each line of *The Art of War* followed by the parallel line in *The Warrior's Apprentice*. This reading changes the context of Sun Tzu's lesson so that trainees can begin to master the magic of strategy by practicing it in meeting their everyday challenges.

As a simple guide to the power of strategy, this book can transform your life. It gives you a new way of perceiving the world and understanding your possibilities and the opportunities that are waiting for you.

Buy it today and study it forever!

Art of War Gift Books

Mastering Strategy Series

^{Sun Tzu's} The Art of War Plus The Warrior's Apprentice
A first book on strategy for the novice.

^{Sun Tzu's} The Art of War Plus The Ancient Chinese Revealed
See the original! Each original Chinese character individually translated.

^{Sun Tzu's} The Art of War Plus Its Amazing Secrets
Learn the hidden secrets! The deeper meaning of Sun Tzu explained.

The Warrior Class: 306 Lessons in Strategy
The complete study guide! Simple lessons in strategy you can read any time.

Career and Business Series

^{Sun Tzu's} The Art of War Plus The Art of Career Building
For everyone! Use Sun Tzu's lessons to advance your career.

^{Sun Tzu's} The Art of War Plus The Art of Sales
For salespeople! Use Sun Tzu's lessons to win sales and keep customers.

^{Sun Tzu's} The Art of War Plus The Art of Management
For managers! Use Sun Tzu's lessons on managing teams more effectively.

^{Sun Tzu's} The Art of War Plus Strategy for Sales Managers
For sales managers! Use Sun Tzu's lessons to direct salespeople more effectively.

^{Sun Tzu's} The Art of War Plus The Art of Small Business
For business owners! Use Sun Tzu's lessons in building your own business.

^{Sun Tzu's} The Art of War Plus The Art of Marketing
For marketing professionals! Use Sun Tzu's lessons to win marketing warfare.

Life Strategies Series

^{Sun Tzu's} The Art of War Plus The Art of Love
For lifelong love! *Bing-fa* applied to finding, winning, and keeping love alive.

^{Sun Tzu's} The Art of War Plus The Art of Parenting Teens
For every parent! Strategy applied to protecting, guiding, and motivating teens.

Current Events Series

^{Sun Tzu's} The Art of War Plus Strategy against Terror
An examination of the War on Terror using Sun Tzu's timeless principles.

Audio and Video

Amazing Secrets of *The Art of War*: Audio
1 1/2 Hours 2-CD set

Amazing Secrets of *The Art of War*: Video
1 1/2 Hours VHS

孫子兵法

Sun Tzu's
THE
ART
OF
WAR

Plus
Book Series

The Warrior's Apprentice

Your First Guide to the Magic of Strategy

孫子兵法

Sun Tzu's

THE
ART
OF
WAR

Plus
Book Series

The Warrior's
Apprentice

Your First Guide to the Magic of Strategy

by Gary Gagliardi

Clearbridge Publishing

Published by
Clearbridge Publishing

FIRST EDITION
Copyright 1999, 2005 Gary Gagliardi

Printed in China.
Interior and cover graphic design for Art of War Plus Book Series by Dana and Jeff Wincapaw.
Original Chinese calligraphy by Tsai Yung, Green Dragon Arts, www.greendragonarts.com.

Publisher's Cataloging-in-Publication Data
Sun-tzu, 6th cent. B.C.
    [Sun-tzu ping fa, English]
    The warrior's apprentice / Gary Gagliardi; Sun Tzu;
    p. 192 cm. 14
 Library of Congress Catalog Card Number: 2005900951
 ISBN 1-929194-32-3 (paperback)
        1. Military art and science - Early works to 1800. 2. Competition. I. Gagliardi, Gary 1951—. II. Title.
U101'.S9513 2005
355'.02 — dc19

Clearbridge Publishing's books may be purchased for business, for any promotional use, or for special sales. Please contact:

Clearbridge Publishing
PO Box 33772, Seattle, WA 98133
Phone: (206)533-9357 Fax: (206)546-9756
www.clearbridge.com

Contents

The Art of War Plus
The Warrior's Apprentice

"The difference between a warrior and an ordinary person is that the warrior sees everything as a challenge while an ordinary person sees everything as a blessing or a curse."

A Separate Reality
Carlos Castaneda

Introduction

Strategy: The Secret Art

Strategy is the most secret art. In ancient China, knowledge about strategy was protected. For over 2,000 years, common people who learned its secrets were destroyed. Today, the power of strategy remains a secret. Everyone uses the word "strategy," but few really know what it means. Strategy isn't planning. Having a strategy isn't like having a good idea. Even world leaders and news commentators are often ignorant about the rules of strategy and how they work.

The rules of strategy were first written down 2,500 hundred years ago in a book that today we call *The Art of War*. However, this book wasn't written to be easy to understand. It was written in a type of code to protect its secrets. For readers who didn't know the key principles of strategy, the book was designed to be confusing and contradictory.

The Art of War wasn't written about war. In reading *The Art of War*, you won't learn how wars were fought in ancient China. You won't know whether its ancient armies used clubs or machine guns. Though written in military terms, the book teaches strategy in its purest form. In Chinese, its title is 兵*bing-*法*fa. Bing-fa* literally means "martial art." Its principles are the basis for all the other martial arts that we know today. Sun Tzu wrote generally about all struggles within society and between people. In discussing these contests, he teaches the use of only one weapon—the most powerful weapon of all—the human mind.

The Power of Strategy

Sun Tzu lived 2,500 years ago. This was before the country that we now call China existed. Hundreds of independent cities occupied the region, much like the city-states of ancient Greece. Each city struggled against its neighbors for local dominance. Sun Tzu saw that most of the efforts in this struggle were wasted and damaging. As an alternative, he developed the art of strategy.

During his lifetime, Sun Tzu used strategy to make the city-state for which he fought, Wu, into the dominant state in the Yellow River valley. Several hundred years later, Sun Tzu's descendant, Sun Ping, taught these secrets to a man named Ying Zheng. This man became the ruler of Qin, and he led his people to conquer all of China. Ying changed his name to Qin Shi Huangdi and became the first emperor of China. Our name for China comes from "Qin," which is pronounced "chin" in English.

It took over two thousand years for the secrets of strategy to reach Europe. A French Jesuit missionary was the first European to translate Sun Tzu's work. It was published in Paris in 1783. A young corporal in the French army read it. This corporal wasn't French—he was an Italian from the island of Corsica—but he soon rose to become the head of the French army. Later, he became the head of the French government. Eventually, he conquered all of continental Europe. His name was Napoleon Bonaparte. Unfortunately, he didn't completely understand Sun Tzu's message, which is why he eventually lost his empire.

The Magic of Positioning

Why is Sun Tzu's strategy so powerful? Sun Tzu saw that our instincts are all wrong. When people are challenged, they react in one of two ways. Sometimes, they run away. Psychologists call this the "flight reflex." Other times, people attack those who threaten them. Psychologists call this the "fight reflex." Sun Tzu saw that neither flight (running away from challenges) nor fight (getting into battles) is successful over the long run.

Instead of flight or fight, strategy teaches the magic of positioning. You have a unique position in the world. Because of that position, you have certain unique advantages and disadvantages. Once you understand your position, you can see opportunities that are available to no one else. Instead of fighting people, you move around them. Instead of running away from challenges, you seek to understand the opportunity that they represent. As you master the techniques of positioning, you constantly move toward your goals, avoiding situations in which you must fight or run away.

People misunderstand the true nature of success. Success doesn't come from size, muscles, or money. It comes from using your position. Instead of thinking about your opponents, you must focus on the potential in your situation. Instead of fighting, strategy teaches you how to advance your position so that people cannot fight you—and ideally, over time, want to join you.

Strategically, both victory and defeat are similar. Each puts you in a new position. When you win your heart's desire—a prize, a love, or a promotion—you always discover that your real challenges are just beginning. Even when you fail to reach your goals, the knowledge you gain from the failure improves your position. Happiness never comes from where you are. The key to happiness is constantly making progress toward the horizon of your goals.

In martial arts, you don't simply push or strike your opponents, because if you do they will simply push and strike back. Instead, you examine your opponents' position. You look for opportunities to use your opponents' apparent strengths against them by catching them out of position. The use of physical leverage in martial art is exactly the same as the use of strategy in everyday life.

The secret is that strategy is a process, not a plan. It is a way of reacting, not an idea. Sun Tzu taught that planning alone does not work because the world is too complex, fast-changing, and unpredictable for rigid, long-term plans. Instead, strategy is a system for creating results under a wide variety of different circumstances. This requires the "warrior's mind," which uses a clear framework for resolving complex situations and choosing the right responses.

With the warrior's mind, you see the world in a different way. You recognize opportunities where you once saw problems. You look for answers instead of blaming others for your problems. When you are faced with a challenge, you can quickly analyze the threat, spot an opening, and act on your instincts.

The secret to strategic success is not just winning battles. It is developing positions that enable you to win without fighting battles. Battles are expensive. If you can advance your position quickly and economically without fighting, you are much better off. As you advance your position, strategy teaches you how to hold on to what you have won. You must be wary of "victories" that consume your time and energy but that fail to position you for long-term success.

The Hidden Code

As we said, *The Art of War* is written in a type of code. Half of this code is subtly revealed in the book's first chapter. There Sun Tzu explains the five key factors that define a strategic position. Then he says that deception is the basis of all warfare, signaling the reader that to understand the rest of the book, he or she must utilize those five key factors.

When you use the five-factors code to decipher the book, you unlock a second code. This secondary code consists of the four steps that Sun Tzu teaches to advance a strategic position. Unlike the five factors, Sun Tzu never mentions these four steps directly, nor does he list them together. You must analyze the original Chinese, using the five factors to discover them. Together, the five factors and four steps decipher a deeper, clearer message in the text.

Your True Position

Before you can get where you are going, you must first know where you are. You use the five key factors to analyze your position and the positions of others. This strategic analysis is the topic of Sun Tzu's first chapter. These five factors are the "dimensions" that characterize a strategic position. These five dimensions are 1) your philosophy, 2) the changing climate, 3) the physical battleground, 4) your character, and 5) your abilities.

Your position is anchored by a core philosophy. Your philosophy defines your purpose or mission. A sense of purpose determines the way you see the world. Sun Tzu teaches that a warrior's philosophy unites him or her with others. Without a core philosophy that you share with others, you are isolated, alone, and strategically weak.

There are different levels of philosophy. Some philosophies are economic. People work with others only to get rewarded. Self-improvement is the basis for higher-level missions. Some individuals focus on developing their personal skills and knowledge. Many warriors work on this level. The most powerful philosophies are based on improving the world. In real war, people don't sacrifice their lives for money or self-improvement but because some ideals, such as freedom and democracy, are more important to them.

The next two dimensions of your strategic position describe your place in the world physically, in both time and space. Strategically, your environment has two opposite and yet complementary halves: the changing climate and the competitive ground. These two elements together mark your unique physical position. No one else can occupy the space you do at the same time.

Strategically, the changing climate is all the forces in nature and society that you cannot control. The weather and the seasons are natural examples of climate. The attitudes and beliefs of people around you are examples of the social climate. Though you cannot control climate, you can learn to use it to your advantage. Climate

孫子兵法

is controlled by time. The first rule of the climate is that it changes. A warrior does not fight against change. Instead, the warrior is trained to see change as the source of all opportunities.

The next dimension of your position is the ground where you choose to compete. This ground supports you and is the source of the rewards you seek. People compete in many different areas—in sports, in business, in academics, socially, in politics, and so on. Each provides a different form of support. The nature of that ground determines how you can advance your position. The ground is connected with the climate. When you choose a competitive arena, you also choose the climate associated with that ground.

Your personality and abilities also define your strategic position. Different people in similar physical circumstances have very different internal resources. Two opposite and complementary elements define your competitive potential: your character and your abilities.

Your character is the dimension of your strategic position that determines how well you make decisions. Sun Tzu calls this leadership. Warriors value five qualities—intelligence, courage, trustworthiness, discipline, and caring. These five character traits determine leadership ability. Warriors are not simply followers. To take the lead, you must have the intelligence and courage to make your own decisions. Others will trust you as a leader only if you demonstrate self-discipline and caring.

The last of the five factors defining your strategic position is ability, or what Sun Tzu calls methods. Ability comes from training. Sun Tzu defines strategy itself as an ability that results from training. While character is the realm of the individual, abilities or methods are the realm of group action. Your abilities define how well you work with others. Warriors realize that they cannot be successful in a vacuum. As Sun Tzu says, strategy depends on people, both understanding them and working with them.

These five factors together—your philosophy, the climate, the ground, your character, and your abilities—define your strategic position. They also determine how to advance a position over time.

Irresistible Force

Positions are not fixed in stone. Positions are dynamic. They are constantly changing. Time naturally erodes your position. If you do nothing to improve your situation, it will tend to get worse. Sun Tzu's first chapter is dedicated to analyzing your position. The next twelve chapters teach you how to defend and advance your position.

The four steps that strategy teaches to advance a position can overcome any obstacle. The strategic process creates an irresistible force. These four steps are 1) learning, 2) seeing, 3) moving, and 4) positioning. They represent a cycle, in which the last step of positioning leads to more learning, triggering another cycle of advance.

Each step in this cycle is intimately connected with the factors that define a strategic position. The basis of learning is the ground. Your competitive arena teaches you what you need to know. The basis of seeing is your character. Your individuality allows you to see certain opportunities. The basis of moving is the climate. The climate provides a window of opportunity for you to act. Finally, your abilities provide the basis of positioning. Your abilities allow you to defend and reap the rewards from your new position.

These four steps advance your position. For example, say you have a problem with someone at work or in your personal life. Sun Tzu teaches that the first step in transforming the situation is learning more about that person. As you learn more, you will see an opening, an opportunity to improve your relationship. For example, you might discover a common interest or a common enemy. Once you discover the opportunity, you have to act on it. That is, you have to change your position. Strategy teaches that you control the positions of others by shifting your own position, not by trying to move them directly. Finally, you have to evaluate whether or not your new position is more rewarding, and, if so, build on it.

These four steps create an endless cycle of improving your position. Learning more about your situation leads to seeing more opportunities. Seeing opportunities requires making decisions about whether to pursue them or not. Pursuing opportunities commits you to new positions that you must defend. These new positions become the launching point for a new cycle of advance.

Strategy teaches that small steps are the most powerful. Most of your advances should be small, quick, and seemingly minor. Over time, however, these little changes make a huge difference. You only need to make major changes in your position if you have made a major mistake. Small changes are much less risky and much more certain over time.

Invincible Strength

As you advance your position, you must maintain your strength. Sun Tzu defines strength as unity and focus, not size and power. Change naturally creates divisions among people, undermining unity. Change also makes it very difficult to maintain your focus. Both unity and focus arise from a shared philosophy and from an underlying concept we might call "oneness." Oneness means being complete or whole. Without this characteristic, you are alienated from those who are important to you. You get confused about the direction of your life.

On the group level, this oneness is the source of team unity. Unity is measured by how readily one member of a team relies on another. Warriors understand that a range of talent is more power-ful than any single individual's talent. Without this underlying solidarity, teams are easily broken. Unity arises from the shared spirit that binds a team together, which is based on the core shared philosophy. Without shared goals, groups are quickly fragmented.

As you advance your position, philosophy makes up the stable core of your strategic position. As your position changes, the other four dimensions that define your strategic position evolve. The climate shifts. You win more ground. Your character develops. You learn more abilities. Amidst these changes, only your philosophy remains stable. Because of its stability, philosophy is the source of trust and faith that binds groups together.

A clear philosophy generates a different form of oneness on a personal level. It creates single-mindedness. When you have a clear mission or purpose, you never lose sight of your goal. You know what you want to achieve.

Another way to describe single-mindedness is focus. Regular people are not very successful because their focus wavers. They leave openings when their attention drifts. Warriors can spot and use those openings. Focus brings together all your resources at a specific time and place. This concentration of effort is the real source of power, according to the principles of strategy. This idea is familiar to anyone who has studied any physical martial art. In martial arts, the whole body concentrates on the point of attack.

Together, the oneness of unity and focus are the source of strength. In many ways, Sun Tzu wrote his work to counter the idea that strength comes from size, wealth, or even position. Most aspects of your position are external and temporary. Though the external dimensions of a position can contribute to your strength, it is your internal strength that matters in the long run.

How to Read This Book

Familiarity with the five key factors that define a position and the four steps that advance a position will help you understand the lessons of *The Art of War*. However, even with this basic understanding, much of the text is still hidden for the uninitiated.

For example, Sun Tzu often talks about "battle," "conflict," and "attack." In English, all these words are closely related, even interchangeable, but in *The Art of War*, these concepts are very different. "Attack" means moving into a new territory—sometimes to hamper another's advance, but not necessarily meeting an opponent. "Battle" means meeting an enemy or a challenge, but it doesn't necessarily mean conflict. "Conflict" is a destructive, hostile confrontation and the least desirable of the three actions.

Though we could spend a lot of time explaining how to decipher all the ideas in Sun Tzu's work (and we do in another book, *The Art of War Plus Its Amazing Secrets*), our goal in this work is to make it easy to use the magic of strategy in your life. To do this, we have decoded Sun Tzu's text in a very simple way.

The Warrior's Apprentice completes *The Art of War* so you can easily understand Sun Tzu's real meaning. We did not want to rewrite or obscure the original *The Art of War*, so we show a complete translation of Sun Tzu's original text on the left-hand pages. However, on the facing right-hand *Warrior's Apprentice* pages, we decode each line so you can use its ideas easily.

The simplest way to read this book is to read each line of *The Art of War*, followed by the parallel line in *The Warrior's Apprentice*. This deciphers the text so that even the uninitiated can use the magic of strategy easily.

In addition, we designed this book like a kaleidoscope so that it can be read in different ways to show different aspects of Sun Tzu's strategic principles. Reading one line at a time is the simplest, but when you read *The Art of War* one stanza or one page at a time, followed by the corresponding sections of *The Warrior's Apprentice*, you discover different shades of meaning.

As an introduction to the power of strategy, this book is the first step in developing the mind of a true warrior.

✦ ✦ ✦

"The path of the Warrior is lifelong, and mastery is often simply staying on the path."

In Search of the Warrior Spirit
Richard Strozzi-Heckler

Chapter 1

Analysis: The Skill of Prophecy

The magic of strategy is that it gives you a framework for understanding the world and predicting the future. Since the world is complex and confusing, this first chapter gives you some simple tools to help you see what is coming. Instead of running away from apparent problems or getting into unnecessary fights with people, warriors must make no assumptions about their position in the world. The skill of prophecy comes from careful analysis.

In his first chapter, Sun Tzu divides the warrior's world into five key components. You use this framework to understand your position in the world and your possibilities.

Sun Tzu then divides society into two types of people. There are warriors, who constantly question their situation. Then there are regular people, who simply never question their assumptions. Warriors open themselves up to outside viewpoints. They listen to others. They ask for help. They work to get to the truth.

Warriors know that they cannot simply trust words or even actions at face value. Appearances are deceptive. Everyone controls how he or she looks to others. To be a warrior, you must learn to see through the illusions of the world.

Strategic analysis comes down to gathering verifiable facts and putting them together logically. Our desires and fears mislead us. Instead of acting out of emotion, we must learn analysis so we can understand where we can succeed.

Analysis

NOTE: *You can read this book horizontally or vertically.*

SUN TZU SAID:

This is war. 1
It is the most important skill in the nation.
It is the basis of life and death.
It is the philosophy of survival or destruction.
You must know it well.

[6]Your skill comes from five factors.
Study these factors when you plan war.
You must insist on knowing your situation.
1. Discuss philosophy.
2. Discuss the climate.
3. Discuss the ground.
4. Discuss leadership.
5. Discuss military methods.

[14]It starts with your military philosophy.
Command your people in a way that gives them a higher
shared purpose.
You can lead others to death.
You can lead others to life.
They must never fear danger or dishonesty.

The Skill of Prophecy

NOTE: *Read a line across both pages at once or down each page separately.*

A WARRIOR HEARS:

1 This is the warrior's way.
You must master the skills of meeting challenges.
These skills are the difference between feeling alive and feeling dead.
These skills are the difference between success and failure.
You must master the magic of strategy.

Your strategic position is defined by five characteristics.
You think about all five aspects when you face a challenge.
Ask these questions to understand your position.
1. What is your purpose?
2. How is your situation changing?
3. Where can you make progress?
4. What is your character?
5. What abilities do you have?

You must know what you believe about your life's purpose.
You can win respect from others only on the basis of sharing their goals and ideals.
Some values are worth dying for.
Some values make life worth living.
The right beliefs protect you from threats and deception.

[19]Next, you have the climate.
It can be sunny or overcast.
It can be hot or cold.
It includes the timing of the seasons.

[23]Next is the terrain.
It can be distant or near.
It can be difficult or easy.
It can be open or narrow.
It also determines your life or death.

[28]Next is the commander.
He must be smart, trustworthy, caring, brave, and strict.

[30]Finally, you have your military methods.
They include the shape of your organization.
They come from your management philosophy.
You must master their use.

[34]All five of these factors are critical.
As a commander, you must pay attention to them.
Understanding them brings victory.
Ignoring them means defeat.

You must see how your world is changing.
Your future can temporarily look bright or dismal.
Your luck will temporarily run hot and cold.
However, everything changes in cycles of time.

You must know how to pick your battles.
You can choose long-term or short-term goals.
Your choices determine how hard or easy your life is.
You can choose broad or specific targets.
Picking the right battles also determines your success or failure.

Next, you must accept responsibility.
Be wise, dependable, sensitive, courageous, and disciplined.

Finally, you need to develop specific abilities and talents.
These skills determine how well you work with others.
Your skills arise from what you really believe is important in life.
You need to train yourself to be successful.

Every one of these five facts is important to your success.
They are what create your opportunities.
If you accept your situation, you will be successful.
If you deny your situation, you will be a failure.

You must learn through planning. 2
You must question the situation.

³You must ask:
Which government has the right philosophy?
Which commander has the skill?
Which season and place has the advantage?
Which method of command works?
Which group of forces has the strength?
Which officers and men have the training?
Which rewards and punishments make sense?
This tells when you will win and when you will lose.

Some commanders perform this analysis.
If you use these commanders, you will win.
Keep them.
Some commanders ignore this analysis.
If you use these commanders, you will lose.
Get rid of them.

Plan an advantage by listening. 3
Adjust to the situation.
Get assistance from the outside.
Influence events.
Then planning can find opportunities and give you control.

2 Warriors learn from strategic analysis.
You must question your assumptions.

You must always be wondering:
Which group has the most powerful philosophy?
How good am I at making decisions?
When and where are my best opportunities?
How well do I communicate with others?
What groups of people will support me?
What leaders and companions can I learn from?
What rewards are worth the risks?
This simple analysis tells you if you are headed for success or failure.

Warriors are those who are willing to question their position.
If you spend your time with these warriors, you will be successful.
Stay with them.
Ordinary people are unwilling to question their position.
If you follow the mindless crowd, you will fail.
Avoid the thoughtless.

3 Warriors discover opportunities by listening to others.
Act on reality, not your limited perceptions.
Seek help from those with an outside viewpoint.
Control what happens in your life.
This is how you discover your options and create your future.

Warfare is one thing. 4
It is a philosophy of deception.

³When you are ready, you try to appear incapacitated.
When active, you pretend inactivity.
When you are close to the enemy, you appear distant.
When far away, you pretend you are near.

⁷You can have an advantage and still entice an opponent.
You can be disorganized and still be decisive.
You can be ready and still be preparing.
You can be strong and still avoid battle.
You can be angry and still stop yourself.
You can humble yourself and still be confident.
You can be relaxed and still be working.
You can be close to an ally and still part ways.
You can attack a place without planning to do so.
You can leave a place without giving away your plan.

¹⁷You will find a place where you can win.
You cannot first signal your intentions.

4 A warrior's way is one thing.
It is the path through the world's illusions.

People will act confident when they are insecure.
People can seem lazy when they are struggling.
People can pretend to be concerned when they are uncaring.
People can appear indifferent when they are worried.

When people tempt you, you must suspect their motives.
Apparently clear-thinking people can be confused.
Seemingly well-equipped people can be poorly prepared.
Those who avoid a fight can be very strong.
Those who appear indifferent can be very emotional.
Those who feign self-assurance can be frightened.
People can work very hard to appear easygoing.
People can be good friends but compete with one another.
People can use opportunities without creating them.
Your direction is not determined by where you come from.

The world offers you plenty of opportunities.
You must be careful of the messages you send.

Manage to avoid battle until your organization can count **5** on certain victory.
You must calculate many advantages.
Before you go to battle, your organization's analysis can indicate that you may not win.
You can count few advantages.
Many advantages add up to victory.
Few advantages add up to defeat.
How can you know your advantages without analyzing them?
We can see where we are by means of our observations.
We can foresee our victory or defeat by planning.

5 Warriors are patient enough to wait until the odds are all in their favor.

You must choose a path that offers many opportunities.

If your success is uncertain, prior analysis of the five factors will predict the problem.

You must avoid paths that offer few opportunities.

Paths with many opportunities lead to success.

Paths with few opportunities lead to failure.

How can you see your path objectively without doing the work?

Warriors train themselves to see their situation as it truly is.

This is how the skill of prophecy creates success and prevents failure.

Chapter 2

Going to War: The Choice of Paths

In his second chapter, Sun Tzu teaches you about price of failure. When you seek to advance your position in a challenging world, your actions cost time and energy. These resources are limited. The magic of strategy is that it enables you, by making the right choices, to avoid wasting time and energy.

This chapter begins by discussing the price of failure. The warrior's way is not painless. Warriors realize that every choice they make has a cost attached to it. Regular people are blissfully unaware of the costs of their decisions. As a warrior's apprentice, you must learn to appreciate the harsh reality of unavoidable costs in the face of limited resources.

Sun Tzu's strategy balances costs with potential rewards. Sun Tzu teaches an economics of conservation. A warrior learns to evaluate every potential move based on its investment in size, time, and space. The bigger, more time-consuming, and more distant an opportunity is, the most costly and risky it is. For this reason, Sun Tzu teaches you to move forward in small, quick, local advances. Small steps are more powerful because they are less risky.

The second part of choosing the right path is identifying opportunities that return more than they consume. Some paths can save you effort, time, and distance. You can identify and put your efforts into activities that increase your capabilities and resources over time. Warriors invest today in efforts that make them more powerful tomorrow.

Going to War

SUN TZU SAID:

Everything depends on your use of military philosophy. 1
Moving the army requires thousands of vehicles.
These vehicles must be loaded thousands of times.
The army must carry a huge supply of arms.
You need ten thousand acres of grain.
This results in internal and external shortages.
Any army consumes resources like an invader.
An army uses up glue and paint for wood.
An army requires armor for its vehicles.
People complain about the waste of a vast amount of metal.
It will set you back when you attempt to raise tens of thousands of troops.

[12]Using a huge army makes war very expensive to win.
Long delays create a dull army and sharp defeats.
Attacking enemy cities drains your forces.
Long violent campaigns that exhaust the nation's resources are wrong.

The Choice of Paths

1 Warriors change everything by the choices they make.
You move forward choosing among thousands of possibilities.
You make thousands of choices about which paths to take.
Your choices can require tremendous amounts of time and effort.
You need enough resources to satisfy your needs.
Your mental and physical assets are limited.
Any endeavor can demand more than it is worth.
Constructing positions requires connections and artifice.
Your existing position requires protection as you move forward.
You have to worry about what every effort will cost you.
Putting your energy into excessive efforts consumes more resources
than these efforts can return.

Size is the first form of cost that makes success more unlikely.
Large projects require preparation that slows your progress.
Setting oversized goals just saps your energy.
Conflicts that consume your limited time and resources lead only to
your failure.

¹⁶You can control a dull army.
You will suffer sharp defeats.
You can drain your forces.
Your money will be used up.
Your rivals will multiply as your army collapses, and they will
begin against you.
It doesn't matter how smart you are.
You cannot get ahead by taking losses!

²³You hear of people going to war too quickly.
Still, you won't see a skilled war that lasts a long time.

²⁵You can fight a war for a long time or you can make your
nation strong.
You can't do both.

Make no assumptions about all the dangers in using 2
military force.
Then you won't make assumptions about the benefits of
using arms either.

³You want to make good use of war.
Do not raise troops repeatedly.
Do not carry too many supplies.
Choose to be useful to your nation.
Feed off the enemy.
Make your army carry only the provisions it needs.

Oversized goals lead to stagnation.

The larger your failure, the more painful it is.

You can expend all your reserves.

Your can overstretch your resources.

This just creates a whole new set of problems, stopping your progress and inviting disaster.

You must avoid getting in over your head.

You cannot succeed by risking everything.

You can jump at an opportunity without enough preparation.

But large investments of time are always costly to your success.

You can invest in long, drawn-out campaigns or you can advance with quick moves forward.

Wasting time makes steady progress impossible.

2 Warriors never pretend that they know all the risks in choosing a course of action.

Because you cannot know all the costs in advance, you cannot know your eventual rewards either.

You must invest your efforts wisely.

You cannot afford to constantly correct your mistakes.

Plan to use small steps forward.

Pick projects that are certain to improve your position.

Use everything others give you.

Plan your progress to maintain the resources you need.

The nation impoverishes itself shipping to troops that **3**
are far away.
Distant transportation is costly for hundreds of families.
Buying goods with the army nearby is also expensive.
High prices also exhaust wealth.
If you exhaust your wealth, you then quickly hollow out your
military.
Military forces consume a nation's wealth entirely.
War leaves households in the former heart of the nation
with nothing.

[8]War destroys hundreds of families.
Out of every ten families, war leaves only seven.
War empties the government's storehouses.
Broken armies will get rid of their horses.
They will throw down their armor, helmets, and arrows.
They will lose their swords and shields.
They will leave their wagons without oxen.
War will consume 60 percent of everything you have.

Because of this, it is the intelligent commander's duty to **4**
feed off the enemy.

[2]Use a cup of the enemy's food.
It is worth twenty of your own.
Win a bushel of the enemy's feed.
It is worth twenty of your own.

3 Warriors who move too far from what they know find that they are poorer for it.

Distance is another form of cost that makes success unlikely.

The further you go, the higher the price you must pay.

You cannot afford the cost of far-flung projects.

The efforts you put into traveling cannot also be used to build up your position.

Moving too far afield can destroy your position completely.

Long-distance campaigns erode dependable forms of support and erode your position.

The life of the warrior is inherently dangerous.

Many attempts at advancing your position are doomed to fail.

Every attempt at moving forward is costly.

Don't risk your future mobility on the possibility of failure.

You must maintain sources of support to defend your position.

Warriors always know how to hold onto their assets.

Warriors always protect their ability to move.

Warriors keep advances small, quick, and local to minimize costs.

4 Warriors maintain their resources through campaigns that return more than they consume.

You can win more time.

An hour spent today can save twenty hours in the future.

You can leverage your finances.

Invest a dollar today to save twenty dollars in the future.

[6]You can kill the enemy and frustrate him as well.
Take the enemy's strength from him by stealing away his
money.

[8]Fight for the enemy's supply wagons.
Capture his supplies by using overwhelming force.
Reward the first who capture them.
Then change their banners and flags.
Mix them in with your own wagons to increase your supply
line.
Keep your soldiers strong by providing for them.
This is what it means to beat the enemy while you grow
more powerful.

Make victory in war pay for itself. 5
Avoid expensive, long campaigns.
The military commander's knowledge is the key.
Knowledge determines if the civilian officials can govern.
Knowledge determines if the nation's households are peace-
ful or a danger to the state.

♦ ♦ ♦

You can improve your situation and gain resources as well.
Address the difficulties that steal away your resources and weaken
your position.

Choose the types of challenges that win you more resources.
Concentrate your efforts on winning new sources of support.
When people give you resources, you must always reward them.
You must identify and organize your resources.
You want to build up your existing resources by continually adding
new ones.
A lack of resources divides people and destroys their strength.
Warriors advance their positions in ways that give them more
resources to draw upon.

5 Warriors recognize progress by how it increases their abilities.
Make the least costly choices to move toward your goals.
The key to cost control is having the right information.
You must know how to support yourself to control your life.
Information is what allows you to reap the rewards of progress and
avoid the costs of conflict.

Chapter 3

Planning an Attack: The Power of Fellowship

Warriors realize that their success always depends on other people. The magic of strategy requires an understanding of human psychology, especially how people act in groups. For Sun Tzu, group psychology is closely tied to philosophy because a shared philosophy is what binds groups together.

In this chapter's first section, Sun Tzu discusses how unity creates success. The goal of unity—and focusing on the tasks at hand—is not to win confrontations but to develop positions that others do not want to attack.

Sun Tzu lists the ways that you can deal with groups of opponents. Sun Tzu lists these measures in the order of their effectiveness. He warns against the worst way of dealing with rivals: attacking them when they are concentrated in a large group.

Strategy teaches the strategic approach to success in the face of opposition: using small, focused engagements in which your group has a clear advantage. He explains how the relative size of competing groups determines the type of engagements you want to create.

The topic then changes to how political divisions undermine the strength of a group. A divided group loses its focus and the result is disastrous. All groups need clear leaders.

Group leaders need certain types of knowledge and skill to make good decisions. You must join groups with good leadership. Leaders are judged by how well they know their teammates, their opponents, their competitive area, and the trends of the climate.

Planning an Attack

SUN TZU SAID:

Everyone relies on the arts of war. 1
A united nation is strong.
A divided nation is weak.
A united army is strong.
A divided army is weak.
A united force is strong.
A divided force is weak.
United men are strong.
Divided men are weak.
A united unit is strong.
A divided unit is weak.

[12]Unity works because it enables you to win every battle you
fight.
Still, this is the foolish goal of a weak leader.
Avoid battle and make the enemy's men surrender.
This is the right goal for a superior leader.

The best way to make war is to ruin the enemy's plans. 2
The next best is to disrupt alliances.
The next best is to attack the opposing army.
The worst is to attack the enemy's cities.

The Power of Fellowship

THE WARRIOR HEARS:

1 Even regular people understand the power of groups.
Being part of a unified group makes you feel secure.
Being part of a group that is divided makes you insecure.
When unified, a group is focused on its external goals.
When divided, a group is pulled in different directions.
When it is focused, a group can advance its position.
When it is confused, a group can lose its position.
When a group improves its position, its members become devoted.
When a group loses its position, its members are dissatisfied.
When a group's members are devoted, they work together well.
When a group's members are dissatisfied, they fight one another.

Regular people join groups because larger groups can consistently
beat smaller ones.
This is not a worthy goal for a warrior.
Warriors seek to succeed by winning over their opposition.
This is why warriors join organizations.

2 Warriors undermine opposition by acting before opponents do.
You can divide opponents by leveraging philosophical differences.
Your group should move against opposing groups only when necessary.
You must never move against an opponent's established position.

[5]This is what happens when you attack a city.
You can attempt it, but you can't finish it.
First you must make siege engines.
You need the right equipment and machinery.
It takes three months and still you cannot win.
Then you try to encircle the area.
You use three more months without making progress.
Your command still doesn't succeed and this angers you.
You then try to swarm the city.
This kills a third of your officers and men.
You are still unable to draw the enemy out of the city.
This attack is a disaster.

Make good use of war. 3
Make the enemy's troops surrender.
You can do this fighting only minor battles.
You can draw the enemy's men out of their cities.
You can do it with small attacks.
You can destroy the men of a nation.
You must keep your campaign short.

[8]You must use total war, fighting with everything you have.
Never stop fighting when at war.
You can gain complete advantage.
To do this, you must plan your strategy of attack.

Opposing groups in a superior position leads to failure.

It is tempting to fight others for choice positions but it never works.

You think you can undermine the strength of their position.

This requires a huge investment of your limited resources.

This futile effort is doomed to waste your time and resources.

You can try to get around a superior position.

You waste more of your time in an effort that gets you nowhere.

You are naturally frustrated, and you are consumed by hostility.

You eventually lash out in rage.

This foolishness costs you many of your supporters and friends.

You cannot displace the opposing groups from their position.

Fighting against established positions is a tragedy.

3 Warriors use their strategic position.

You must know how to win away an opposing group's support.

You do this by advancing your position one small step at a time.

You can lure a group's members away from their position.

You must understand the power of focused attacks.

Over time, your progress can undermine the largest opponents.

You do this a little at a time.

You always work to advance your position, using every opportunity.

It is your persistence that brings you success.

You can overcome any opponent that stands in your way.

Your success depends entirely on choosing methods that work.

[12]The rules for making war are:
If you outnumber enemy forces ten to one, surround them.
If you outnumber them five to one, attack them.
If you outnumber them two to one, divide them.
If you are equal, then find an advantageous battle.
If you are fewer, defend against them.
If you are much weaker, evade them.

[19]Small forces are not powerful.
However, large forces cannot catch them.

You must master command. 4
The nation must support you.

[3]Supporting the military makes the nation powerful.
Not supporting the military makes the nation weak.

[5]The army's position is made more difficult by politicians in
three different ways.
Ignorant of the whole army's inability to advance, they order
an advance.
Ignorant of the whole army's inability to withdraw, they
order a withdrawal.
We call this tying up the army.
Politicians don't understand the army's business.
Still, they think they can run an army.
This confuses the army's officers.

The right methods depend on your group's relative size.
Overwhelming size wins by engulfing opponents.
Dominant size wins by challenging opponents.
Superior size wins by dividing opponents.
Equal size wins by picking challenges that opponents cannot meet.
Smaller size wins by defending well-protected positions.
Insignificant size wins by staying ahead of opponents.

Large groups of people have the advantage of power.
Small groups of people have the advantage of speed.

4 Warriors know how to lead a group.
You must know how to win the support of your companions.

Having the support of others makes you powerful.
Not having the support of others makes you weak.

If you are part of a group in which competing interests influence
decision-making, you must expect certain problems.
Divided groups often act to benefit a part of the group while hurt-
ing the organization as a whole.
Divided groups often act to protect some members to the detriment
of other members.
Internal politics divides many groups.
Politicians destroy every group's focus on its mission.
Politicians have their own agendas.
Politicians make decision-making difficult.

[12]Politicians don't know the army's chain of command.
They give the army too much freedom.
This will create distrust among the army's officers.

[15]The entire army becomes confused and distrusting.
This invites invasion by many different rivals.
We say correctly that disorder in an army kills victory.

You must know five things to win: 5
Victory comes from knowing when to attack and when to avoid battle.
Victory comes from correctly using both large and small forces.
Victory comes from everyone sharing the same goals.
Victory comes from finding opportunities in problems.
Victory comes from having a capable commander and the government leaving him alone.
You must know these five things.
You then know the theory of victory.

We say: 6
"Know yourself and know your enemy.
You will be safe in every battle.
You may know yourself but not know the enemy.
You will then lose one battle for every one you win.
You may not know yourself or the enemy.
You will then lose every battle."

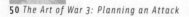

Internal politics confuses a group's priorities.

Without clear priorities, any decision can be defended.

Leaders in a group must have confidence in one another.

A breakdown in a group's unity and focus creates weakness.

Weakness in an organization invites attack.

Without solid leadership, no group can be successful.

5 Warriors understand the basis of their group's position.

You must know how to time your advance based on the changing trends of the climate.

You must know how to judge the relative size and power of opponents and act appropriately.

You must know how to unite groups based on a clear philosophy.

You must discover opportunities by knowing your ground.

You must recognize that groups require a leader and that internal politics weakens a group.

These five factors are the basis of your strategic position.

Join groups only with solid strategic positions.

6 Warriors hear:

You must know what your group and opposing groups can do.

You can then avoid confrontations that are disastrous.

You can easily underestimate your opponent's capabilities.

When you are ignorant, your success is only a matter of chance.

At the same time, you can also overestimate your own capabilities.

When you are arrogant and ignorant, you are doomed.

Chapter 4

Positioning: The Place of Judgment

We could call strategy the lazy person's path to success. The whole purpose of strategy is to find easy ways to achieve your goals and the easiest places that allow you to pursue them.

Real warriors, unlike make-believe warriors, don't go looking for big fights. They don't feel the need to prove to anyone how smart or brave they are. They certainly don't need to do stupid or dangerous things to create the appearance of courage. Warriors don't care about image. They care about what is real.

You make success easy by using your existing position as your springboard to future success. Regular people tend to think negatively about their current situation. This negativity results in a sense of inadequacy and inferiority. Warriors see the unique value in their position. Warriors are keenly aware of their own assets.

If you value your existing position, you will do what you must to protect it. Regular people take their situation for granted. They neglect maintaining what they have. The result is that their situation always tends to get worse. Warriors prize their existing position and defend it fiercely. They realize that their current situation is the core of all their future success.

Without a proper appreciation for what you already have, you cannot move forward. Regular people envy other people's positions and their opportunities. Warriors see that their positions offer the best possible opportunities for them. You can duplicate the methods of others, but you must find your own path.

Positioning

SUN TZU SAID:

Learn from the history of successful battles. 1
Your first actions should deny victory to the enemy.
You pay attention to your enemy to find the way to win.
You alone can deny victory to the enemy.
Only your enemy can allow you to win.

⁶You must fight well.
You can prevent the enemy's victory.
You cannot win unless the enemy enables your victory.

⁹We say:
You see the opportunity for victory; you don't create it.

You are sometimes unable to win. 2
You must then defend.
You will eventually be able to win.
You must then attack.
Defend when you have insufficient strength.
Attack when you have a surplus of strength.

The Place of Judgment

THE WARRIOR HEARS:

1 Observe successful people and copy them.
Your first duty is to protect your existing position.
Study openings that others leave to see your opportunities.
Do not give anyone an opening to attack you.
Wait until others offer you an opening as a path to your success.

Use your efforts wisely.
What you do determines how safe you are.
What other people do determines where your opportunities lie.

Warriors learn.
Open your eyes to see the opportunities that are available to you.

2 You must be patient until you recognize an opportunity.
Protect what you already have.
Time opens up new opportunities.
Take advantage of them without hesitation.
You can build up your abilities while you are waiting.
When you have more abilities, you discover more opportunities.

7You must defend yourself well.
Save your forces and dig in.
You must attack well.
Move your forces when you have a clear advantage.

11You must always protect yourself until you can completely
triumph.

Some may see how to win. 3
However, they cannot position their forces where they must.
This demonstrates limited ability.

4Some can struggle to a victory and the whole world may
praise their winning.
This also demonstrates a limited ability.

6Win as easily as picking up a fallen hair.
Don't use all of your forces.
See the time to move.
Don't try to find something clever.
Hear the clap of thunder.
Don't try to hear something subtle.

12Learn from the history of successful battles.
Victory goes to those who make winning easy.
A good battle is one that you will obviously win.
It doesn't take intelligence to win a reputation.
It doesn't take courage to achieve success.

Always protect your position.
Conserve your resources and keep a low profile.
Always look for opportunities to advance your position.
Wait to move until you know that you can move successfully.

Avoid risking your existing position until you are certain that you can move forward.

3 Some people find it easy to see opportunities.
These people, however, often lack the courage to make a move.
Vision without action gets you nowhere.

Others make the mistake of fighting costly battles that they need luck to win.
Action without judgment also gets you nowhere.

Good strategy teaches you to take small steps forward.
Keep some resources in reserve just in case.
Wait until you have a clear opening.
Don't imagine opportunities where none exist.
Real opportunities are always clear-cut.
Imaginary opportunities are always elusive.

The most lasting progress requires picking the right opportunities.
Warriors are not heroes who look for difficult challenges.
A challenge is worthwhile if it moves you forward easily.
People who fight battles to build a reputation are foolish.
Only fools look for glory at the expense of success.

17You must win your battles without effort.
Avoid difficult struggles.
Fight when your position must win.
You always win by preventing your defeat.

21You must engage only in winning battles.
Position yourself where you cannot lose.
Never waste an opportunity to defeat your enemy.

24You win a war by first assuring yourself of victory.
Only afterward do you look for a fight.
Outmaneuver the enemy before the first battle and then
fight to win.

You must make good use of war. 4
Study military philosophy and the art of defense.
You can control your victory or defeat.

4This is the art of war:
"1. Discuss the distances.
2. Discuss your numbers.
3. Discuss your calculations.
4. Discuss your decisions.
5. Discuss victory.

10The ground determines the distance.
The distance determines your numbers.
Your numbers determine your calculations.
Your calculations determine your decisions.
Your decisions determine your victory."

Strategy is the lazy person's path to success.
Avoid the hard work.
Let your position work for you.
You must never leave openings that others can attack.

Warriors avoid fights they cannot win.
Warriors avoid positions they cannot defend.
You must use every opportunity that comes your way.

Success over the long term requires developing your position.
Choose stepping-stones that make the next step forward easy.
You gradually advance your position to make capturing your next
objective easy.

4 Warriors do not waste their efforts.
You must know what values are worth defending.
Your choices determine what happens to you.

Strategy clearly defines a good opportunity.
1. Opportunities are close to what you already know.
2. Opportunities require the abilities that you have.
3. Opportunities favor you more than someone else.
4. Opportunities offer a minimum of risks.
5. Opportunities position you for future advance.

Your current position generates your knowledge.
Your knowledge creates your abilities.
Your abilities can be compared to the abilities of others.
Comparisons tell you when the odds are in your favor.
Favorable situations open up new opportunities in the future.

[15]Creating a winning war is like balancing a coin of gold
against a coin of silver.
Creating a losing war is like balancing a coin of silver
against a coin of gold.

Winning a battle is always a matter of people.
You pour them into battle like a flood of water pouring into
a deep gorge.
This is a matter of positioning.

♦ ♦ ♦

You can't do everything so you must choose your best options over your second-best options.

Over the long term, investing in second-rate opportunities adds up to failure.

5 Warriors know that their success depends upon other people. You need the overwhelming support of everyone to give your progress real momentum.

Everyone must support the right positions.

Chapter 5

Momentum: The Element of Surprise

How do you meet every challenge so that you are confident you will succeed? You must understand that you never have complete control over your environment. The magic of strategy is that it gives you control over unpredictable situations. To get this control, you use what Sun Tzu calls "momentum."

The term "momentum" has a very specific definition in the science of strategy. In common usage, especially sports, momentum is generally defined by the idea that past success leads to future success. While Sun Tzu would agree that momentum leads to success, he would not agree that success leads to momentum. Instead, true momentum comes from using the element of surprise.

Strategically, surprise is based upon setting expectations. If people don't know what to expect, everything is random so nothing is a surprise. You must have a standard, called direct action, that sets up the surprise or innovation based on creativity.

Innovation requires that you put together common, familiar ideas in new and interesting ways. Dependability is good, but you don't want opponents to know exactly how you will respond. It is the unpredictable that gives you power.

Every strategic encounter will take unexpected turns. The key is to prepare your surprises in advance. A warrior learns how to prepare for changes in direction and to harness them to create momentum. If you are prepared for the unexpected and your opponents are not, you can take control of a confused situation.

Momentum

SUN TZU SAID:

You control a large group the same as you control a few. 1
You just divide their ranks correctly.
You fight a large army the same as you fight a small one.
You only need the right position and communication.
You may meet a large enemy army.
You must be able to sustain an enemy attack without being
defeated.
You must correctly use both surprise and direct action.
Your army's position must increase your strength.
Troops flanking an enemy can smash them like eggs.
You must correctly use both strength and weakness.

It is the same in all battles. 2
You use a direct approach to engage the enemy.
You use surprise to win.

4You must use surprise for a successful invasion.
Surprise is as infinite as the weather and land.
Surprise is as inexhaustible as the flow of a river.

The Element of Surprise

1 Warriors are not intimidated by the size of a challenge.
The secret is breaking tasks down into manageable steps.
You solve large problems by addressing a series of smaller ones.
You advance your position gradually while gathering information.
An unexpected tragedy can blindside you.
If you do not panic, you can survive any setback without being
crushed by it.
You must create expectations but then go beyond what is expected.
You must leverage the resources of your existing position.
You can find surprisingly easy ways around even difficult problems.
Within every problem, you must look for a hidden opportunity.

2 Warriors have a system for meeting challenges.
They always face their problems directly.
They solve their problems creatively.

You improve your position by being creative.
Use your environment and its changes to fuel your ideas.
You will never run out of creative new innovations.

⁷You can be stopped and yet recover the initiative.
You must use your days and months correctly.

⁹If you are defeated, you can recover.
You must use the four seasons correctly.

¹¹There are only a few notes in the scale.
Yet you can always rearrange them.
You can never hear every song of victory.

¹⁴There are only a few basic colors.
Yet you can always mix them.
You can never see all the shades of victory.

¹⁷There are only a few flavors.
Yet you can always blend them.
You can never taste all the flavors of victory.

²⁰You fight with momentum.
There are only a few types of surprises and direct actions.
Yet you can always vary the ones you use.
There is no limit to the ways you can win.

²⁴Surprise and direct action give birth to each other.
They are like a circle without end.
You cannot exhaust all their possible combinations!

Surging water flows together rapidly. 3
Its pressure washes away boulders.
This is momentum.

When you have a setback, you can regain your momentum.
Every new day and new month presents new opportunities.

You can make progress even after a disaster.
You must invest your time in creating new possibilities.

Old ideas may sound tired and familiar.
You spark new ideas by simply playing with old ones.
Everything you hear can be a source of inspiration.

No situation is ever as simple as black and white.
The key to creativity is finding a new point of view.
Your success depends on seeing subtle distinctions.

You have a limited number of ingredients with which to work.
However, there is no limit to how you can put them together.
This is why your human potential is infinite.

Momentum comes from exceeding expectations.
Neither surprising people nor setting expectations is complicated.
People expect you to react as you have before.
By escaping from your habits, you give yourself momentum.

Expectations enable surprise, and surprise changes expectations.
Each element makes the other possible.
Continually shaping expectations makes new surprises possible.

3 The pressure of change comes from its speed.
Continuous change wears away any obstacle.
Momentum depends on change.

⁴A hawk suddenly strikes a bird.
Its contact alone kills the prey.
This is timing.

⁷You must fight only winning battles.
Your momentum must be overwhelming.
Your timing must be exact.

¹⁰Your momentum is like the tension of a bent crossbow.
Your timing is like the pulling of a trigger.

War is very complicated and confusing. 4
Battle is chaotic.
Nevertheless, you must not allow chaos.

⁴War is very sloppy and messy.
Positions turn around.
Nevertheless, you must never be defeated.

⁷Chaos gives birth to control.
Fear gives birth to courage.
Weakness gives birth to strength.

¹⁰You must control chaos.
This depends on your planning.
Your men must brave their fears.
This depends on their momentum.

¹⁴You have strengths and weaknesses.
These come from your position.

The force of surprise comes from its suddenness.
Its revelation alone creates a moment of truth.
Pick the right moment to use it.

You cannot afford to take any challenge lightly.
Momentum must be clearly on your side.
Know exactly when a sudden change is required.

You use the pace of change to pressure opponents.
A sudden surprise collapses that pressure all at once.

4 When opposing plans collide, the result cannot be predicted.
But that confusion creates new opportunities.
Your job is to use random opportunities in a consistent way.

No real-life situation involving other people is clean and simple.
Situations that look bad can turn out to be very good.
As long as you stay in the game, you can make progress.

Only unpredictable change creates major opportunities.
Facing the unknown requires us to make choices.
Warriors recognize their limitations, which enables them to succeed.

You must prepare for confusion.
You must leave room in your plans for the unexpected.
Warriors are not threatened by a surprising development.
They use surprise to increase their momentum.

You must know what you can do and what you cannot do.
As you advance your position, your capabilities will change.

[16]You must force the enemy to move to your advantage.
Use your position.
The enemy must follow you.
Surrender a position.
The enemy must take it.
You can offer an advantage to move him.
You can use your men to move him.
You can use your strength to hold him.

You want a successful battle. 5
To do this, you must seek momentum.
Do not just demand a good fight from your people.
You must pick good people and then give them momentum.

[5]You must create momentum.
You create it with your men during battle.
This is comparable to rolling trees and stones.
Trees and stones roll because of their shape and weight.
Offer men safety and they will stay calm.
Endanger them and they will act.
Give them a place and they will hold.
Round them up and they will march.

[13]You make your men powerful in battle with momentum.
This should be like rolling round stones down over a high,
steep cliff.
Momentum is critical.

✦ ✦ ✦

You need to manipulate your opponents to set up an opportunity.

Act as they expect you to.

They will react based on their assumptions.

Concede to give them confidence.

They will become convinced of their opportunity.

This is how you lure opponents into a bad position.

Your efforts can then make their bad situation worse.

Once they are at a disadvantage, you can keep them in control.

5 Warriors continually advance because they look for challenges.
You must face challenges directly to set up a surprise.

Success is never a matter of just working harder or better.

The best warriors are the least predictable.

You control your momentum.

In the confusion of battle, you must understand how people think.

People act predictably based on their human nature.

People act according to their personality and their self-interest.

If nothing changes, people will do what they have always done.

People will act only if they are afraid of losing something.

People will stand if they have something to defend.

When people are in a group, they follow the example of others.

Warriors know how to succeed by using the element of surprise.

You work to set up a surprise by getting everything in the right position beforehand.

Momentum shifts the situation in your favor.

♦ ♦ ♦

Chapter 6

Weakness and Strength: The Alchemy of Opposites

Strategy requires constantly improving your position. To continually make progress in a competitive world, you must leverage your strengths against your rivals' weaknesses. Sun Tzu teaches the secret for accomplishing this using the alchemy of opposites. The rule of opposites teaches that if you seek out emptiness, you will find fullness, and if you seek out weakness, you will find strength.

The first application of this rule is choosing a battleground. Regular people follow the crowd, so warriors do the opposite. They seek new, unexplored areas.

Emptiness creates speed. Warriors go around obstacles instead of wasting time struggling with them. You want to maintain your opponents' ignorance about your plans, so warriors avoid talking about their goals. Braggarts make themselves easy targets because they are so full of themselves.

Focus or concentration is a form of fullness, while division is a form of emptiness. Everything that is put together from separate parts has seams of emptiness or weakness. You concentrate your efforts at those weak points to generate strength.

Since opposites tend to replace each other, situations are fluid. What was once empty becomes full and what was full is emptied. Warriors change their positions as these shifts warrant. Success goes to those who can adjust to these changes most quickly. Every window of opportunity that opens is open for only a limited time. You must act instantly before others know what you are doing.

Weakness and Strength

SUN TZU SAID:

Always arrive first to the empty battlefield to await the 1
enemy at your leisure.
After the battleground is occupied and you hurry to it,
fighting is more difficult.

3You want a successful battle.
Move your men, but not into opposing forces.

5You can make enemies come to you.
Offer them an advantage.
You can make enemies avoid coming to you.
Threaten them with danger.

9When enemies are fresh, you can tire them.
When they are well fed, you can starve them.
When they are relaxed, you can move them.

The Alchemy of Opposites

THE WARRIOR HEARS:

1 Warriors are pioneers who discover new areas and keep ahead of the crowd.
Regular people follow the crowd and put themselves in constant competition with others.

You want to make progress easily.
You must move forward where other people leave openings.

You sometimes want your rivals to follow your lead.
You must leave an opening for them.
You can also keep your opponents from copying you.
You must deny them any opening.

For everyone, fullness is only a temporary state.
No matter how much people have, they will soon want more.
No matter how comfortable people are, they will soon get restless.

Leave any place without haste. 2
Hurry to where you are unexpected.
You can easily march hundreds of miles without tiring.
To do so, travel through areas that are deserted.
You must take whatever you attack.
Attack when there is no defense.
You must have walls to defend.
Defend where it is impossible to attack.

9Be skilled in attacking.
Give the enemy no idea where to defend.

11Be skillful in your defense.
Give the enemy no idea where to attack.

Be subtle! Be subtle! 3
Arrive without any clear formation.
Ghostly! Ghostly!
Arrive without a sound.
You must use all your skill to control enemies' decisions.

6Advance where they can't defend.
Charge through their openings.
Withdraw where enemies cannot chase you.
Move quickly so that they cannot catch you.

2 Warriors are slow to give up what they have.
However, you must utilize unexpected openings instantly.
If you are going in the right direction, you feel energized.
The right direction always leads away from the crowd.
When you move into new areas, commit yourself to success.
Avoid obstacles that will slow you down.
Establish a strong position when you stake out a claim.
This discourages others from challenging you.

Continually search out new opportunities.
Keep everyone guessing about what you will do next.

Take nothing you have for granted.
Discover your weaknesses before your opponents do.

3 Warriors keep their opponents ignorant.
You must never signal what you intend to accomplish.
Maintain the mystery.
Move into new areas quietly.
Success comes from controlling the perceptions of others.

You make your best progress when you are unopposed.
Windows of opportunity do not remain open.
Move into areas where others cannot go.
You must keep ahead of the crowd.

[10]Always pick your own battles.
Enemies can hide behind high walls and deep trenches.
Do not try to win by fighting them directly.
Instead, attack a place that they must recapture.
Avoid the battles that you don't want.
You can divide the ground and yet defend it.
Don't give enemies anything to win.
Divert them by coming to where you defend.

Make other men take a position while you take none. 4
Then focus your forces where enemies divide their forces.
Where you focus, you unite your forces.
When enemies divide, they create many small groups.
You want your large group to attack one of their small ones.
Then you have many men where enemies have but a few.
Your larger force can overwhelm a small one.
Then go on to the next small enemy group.
You can take them one at a time.

You must keep the place that you have chosen as a 5
battleground a secret.
Enemies must not know it.
Force enemies to prepare their defense in many places.
You want enemies to defend many places.
Then you can choose where to fight.
Their forces will be weak there.

You always have good options.
Some desirable positions are extremely well protected.
Going after these positions is a recipe for failure.
Instead, go after desirable positions that others have ignored.
No one can force you into a fight.
Define your territory in a way that makes it easy to protect.
No one should benefit from attacking you.
Make it clear that there is nothing for them to win.

4 Warriors are flexible while others take rigid positions.
Warriors find the holes in the positions taken by others.
You must concentrate your efforts on one opportunity at a time.
Regular people get scattered among too many areas.
Your concentration on one area makes your rivals easy to beat.
Warriors apply all their resources toward the immediate challenge.
Concentrated efforts succeed where diluted efforts fail.
Tackle small, distracted opponents one after another.
Each small success adds up to progress.

5 Warriors do not talk about where they plan to focus their
efforts next.
Keep your priorities to yourself.
Regular people are unable to decide upon their priorities.
They defend everything they do as important.
Choose challenges that other people avoid.
You will encounter little opposition.

7If they reinforce their front lines, they deplete their rear.
If they reinforce their rear, they deplete their front.
If they reinforce their right flank, they deplete their left.
If they reinforce their left flank, they deplete their right.
Without knowing the place of attack, they cannot prepare.
Without knowing the right place, they will be weak everywhere.

13Your enemies have weak points.
Prepare your men against them.
Your enemies have strong points.
Make their men prepare themselves against you.

You must know the battleground. 6
You must know the time of battle.
You can then travel a thousand miles and still win the battle.

4The enemy should not know the battleground.
He shouldn't know the time of battle.
His left flank will be unable to support his right.
His right will be unable to support his left.
His front lines will be unable to support his rear.
His rear will be unable to support his front.
His support is distant even if it is only ten miles away.
What unknown place can be close?

12You control the balance of forces.
The enemy may have many men but they are superfluous.
How can they help him to victory?

Regular people are always shifting their priorities.
They are easily distracted by every passing fashion.
They jump from one thing to another.
The result is that they are always out of balance.
Regular people never identify what they must focus on.
They never accomplish anything.

Everyone has gaps in his or her abilities.
Target the gaps your opponents leave you.
Everyone excels at some things.
They cannot defend their strengths if you don't attack them.

6 Warriors pick challenges on ground they know.
You must select a time that is in your favor.
You can go any distance when success there is certain.

Focus on situations in which your opponents are poorly informed.
Pick situations in which your opponents are unprepared.
When people are ill informed, they cannot react appropriately.
When people react inappropriately, they get the wrong information.
When situations fail to go as planned, people are taken by surprise.
When people are taken by surprise, no plan can be successful.
Ignorance creates obstacles to every reasonable response.
Ignorance makes every task difficult.

You alone know when and where you must act.
Pick a battle when your opponents' resources are unavailable.
Your knowledge is the key to your success.

[15]We say:
You must let victory happen.

[17]The enemy may have many men.
You can still control him without a fight.

When you form your strategy, know the strengths and 7
weaknesses of your plan.
When you execute a plan, know how to manage both action
and inaction.
When you take a position, know the deadly and the winning
grounds.
When you enter into battle, know when you have too many
or too few men.

[5]Use your position as your war's centerpiece.
Arrive at the battle without a formation.
Don't take a position in advance.
Then even the best spies can't report it.
Even the wisest general cannot plan to counter you.
Take a position where you can triumph using superior numbers.
Keep opposing forces ignorant.
Everyone should learn your location after your position has
given you success.
No one should know how your location gives you a winning
position.
Make a successful battle one from which the enemy cannot
recover.
You must continually adjust your position to his position.

Pay attention.

Pick your opportunities wisely.

It doesn't matter how powerful your opponents are.

They can't fight what they don't understand.

7 Warriors factor in the advantages and disadvantages of their position in planning every move.

No plan is perfect, but you must know when action is better than doing nothing.

No position is perfect, but you must know which directions lead to success and which to failure.

You must choose the challenges that are best suited to your capabilities.

Your strategic position is your central asset.

When meeting a new challenge, wait before committing yourself.

Don't give away your intentions.

Keep your opponents in the dark as long as possible.

Do not give people time to prepare to act against you.

Focus all your efforts on one thing at one time to achieve success.

Don't let others know what to expect.

Others should know where you are headed only after it is too late to stop you.

Others should understand your opportunity only after it is too late to undermine it.

People can hamper your progress only if you give them the opportunity to do so.

You must be faster and more flexible than your opponents.

Manage your military position like water. 8
Water takes every shape.
It avoids the high and moves to the low.
Your war can take any shape.
It must avoid the strong and strike the weak.
Water follows the shape of the land that directs its flow.
Your forces follow the enemy, who determines how you win.

[8]Make war without a standard approach.
Water has no consistent shape.
If you follow the enemy's shifts and changes, you can always
find a way to win.
We call this shadowing.

[12]Fight five different campaigns without a firm rule for victory.
Use all four seasons without a consistent position.
Your timing must be sudden.
A few weeks determine your failure or success.

♦ ♦ ♦

8 Warriors are infinitely adaptable.
You can adjust to every situation.
Find success by following the path of least resistance.
Success can take an infinite number of forms.
You must avoid obstacles and move into openings.
You must understand your position and leverage it.
You embrace problems because they are the source of opportunity.

Your progress will take different forms at different times.
Consistent progress requires constant fine-tuning.
If you have good information, you will inevitably discover oppor-
tunities.
Keep close to good information sources.

In each situation, the critical element can be different.
As you move forward, new possibilities emerge.
Act instantly when you recognize an opportunity.
You can change your situation overnight.

Chapter 7

Armed Conflict: The Suppression of Hostility

Good strategy dictates that you avoid unnecessary conflict because it makes success too costly. The more confrontations you have in life, the less likely your success becomes. However, when confrontations are unavoidable, good strategy positions you to deal with them successfully.

Sun Tzu begins this chapter by explaining that confrontations are best avoided. Your real opportunities lie in taking your own path, distancing yourself from the crowd. This approach naturally avoids most forms of direct confrontation. The focus of strategy is continual progress, not beating others. Speed is important to progress, and confrontations with others only slow you down.

You cannot force a favorable showdown with rivals or opponents. When you obviously want a showdown, your opponents are going to do their best to avoid you. Instead, you must lull opponents into a false sense of security. You confuse the situation so that rivals are unprepared for your opposition.

Communication is often the key to winning unavoidable confrontations. Who wins or loses a confrontation largely depends other people taking sides. The role of good communication is to get as many people on your side as possible.

Warriors choose the right time and place for unavoidable confrontations. You must be patient enough to wait until everything is in your favor. You must also remember that your goal is to remove an opponent as an obstacle, not to make him or her fight you.

Armed Conflict

SUN TZU SAID:

Everyone uses the arts of war. 1
You accept orders from the government.
Then you assemble your army.
You organize your men and build camps.
You must avoid disasters from armed conflict.

[6]Seeking armed conflict can be disastrous.
Because of this, a detour can be the shortest path.
Because of this, problems can become opportunities.

[9]Use an indirect route as your highway.
Use the search for advantage to guide you.
When you fall behind, you must catch up.
When you get ahead, you must wait.
You must know the detour that most directly accomplishes
your plan.

[14]Undertake armed conflict when you have an advantage.
Seeking armed conflict for its own sake is dangerous.

The Suppression of Hostility

THE WARRIOR HEARS:

1 Everyone tries to think strategically.
Everyone has to meet obligations to other people.
Everyone puts together resources.
Everyone organizes his or her efforts and chooses positions.
Warriors alone know how to avoid senseless confrontations.

Only fools go looking for battles to prove themselves.
Going out of your way to avoid fights is the path to success.
Avoiding confrontations uncovers new ways to make progress.

The best way to make progress is to go around opponents.
You must look for opportunities, not showdowns.
Setbacks are temporary nuisances.
Getting ahead of yourself is what is truly dangerous.
You can learn the best way around opponents that stand in your path.

You can fight when you are certain to gain something valuable.
Every fight that cannot be avoided is inherently risky.

You can build up an army to fight for an advantage. 2
Then you won't catch the enemy.
You can force your army to go fight for an advantage.
Then you abandon your heavy supply wagons.

5You keep only your armor and hurry after the enemy.
You avoid stopping day or night.
You use many roads at the same time.
You go hundreds of miles to fight for an advantage.
Then the enemy catches your commanders and your army.
Your strong soldiers get there first.
Your weaker soldiers follow behind.
Using this approach, only one in ten will arrive.
You can try to go fifty miles to fight for an advantage.
Then your commanders and army will stumble.
Using this method, only half of your soldiers will make it.
You can try to go thirty miles to fight for an advantage.
Then only two out of three will get there.

18If you make your army travel without good supply lines,
your army will die.
Without supplies and food, your army will die.
If you don't save the harvest, your army will die.

2 Warriors do not attempt to pursue a decisive showdown.
Your opponents can easily avoid these situations.
It is always a mistake to chase after any confrontation.
Your impatience undermines your support from others.

No armor can defend you from your own impatience.
Speed is dangerous when it wearies you.
Speed is dangerous when it divides you.
Impatience for a showdown tempts you to overextend yourself.
When you are overextended, you are likely to make bad choices.
You may start off strong.
However, you will finish poorly.
Nine times out of ten, overextending yourself leads to failure.
Impatience for a showdown puts you off balance.
Then you are more inclined to make mistakes.
Being off balance always depletes your resources.
Impatience for a showdown takes you out of position.
Being out of position always weakens you.

Warriors don't look for fights when fighting will undermine their
long-term support from others.
Warriors don't look for fights that strain their resources.
Warriors don't look for fights that cannot enrich them.

[21]Do not let any of your potential enemies know what you are planning.

Still, you must not hesitate to form alliances.

You must know the mountains and forests.

You must know where the obstructions are.

You must know where the marshes are.

If you don't, you cannot move the army.

If you don't, you must use local guides.

If you don't, you can't take advantage of the terrain.

You make war by making a false stand. 3

By finding an advantage, you can move.

By dividing and joining, you can reinvent yourself and transform the situation.

You can move as quickly as the wind.

You can rise like the forest.

You can invade and plunder like fire.

You can stay as motionless as a mountain.

You can be as mysterious as the fog.

You can strike like sounding thunder.

[10]Divide your troops to plunder the villages.

When on open ground, dividing is an advantage.

Don't worry about organization; just move.

Be the first to find a new route that leads directly to a winning plan.

This is how you are successful at armed conflict.

You must not let potential opponents think that you want to fight with them.

Instead, your first goal is to make them your friends.

By getting close to them, you learn their strengths and secrets.

You need to know where they might hamper your progress.

You need to learn where you might get stuck.

Without this knowledge, progress is impossible.

To get this information, you need to be close to your enemies.

Use your knowledge to strengthen your position.

3 A warrior's success depends on manipulating appearances.

You must have the patience to uncover the right opportunities.

You can catch your opponents off balance if you can change the way a situation looks.

Use speed to confuse your opponents.

Use surprise to confuse your opponents.

Confusion allows you to move forward and accumulate resources.

Confusion allows you to stand and defend your position.

The secret is keeping your opponents in the dark.

Surprise leads to quick successes.

Misleading opponents allows you to reap many awards at once.

You are left alone when your opponents are confused.

Even when you lack unity, it doesn't hurt you.

A surprise can reveal the easiest way around the obstacles that confront you.

Outmaneuvering opponents enables you to win in confrontations.

Military experience says: 4
"You can speak, but you will not be heard.
You must use gongs and drums.
You cannot really see your forces just by looking.
You must use banners and flags."

6You must master gongs, drums, banners, and flags.
Place people as a single unit where they can all see and hear.
You must unite them as one.
Then the brave cannot advance alone.
The fearful cannot withdraw alone.
You must force them to act as a group.

12In night battles, you must use numerous fires and drums.
In day battles, you must use many banners and flags.
You must position your people to control what they see and
hear.

You control your army by controlling its morale. 5
As a general, you must be able to control emotions.

3In the morning, a person's energy is high.
During the day, it fades.
By evening, a person's thoughts turn to home.
You must use your troops wisely.
Avoid the enemy's high spirits.
Strike when his men are lazy and want to go home.
This is how you master energy.

4 Warriors learn from experience.
You should never expect people to listen to you.
You must work hard to get attention.
You cannot let yourself be confused by complex appearances.
You need a framework for organizing your efforts.

Communication is the key to controlling confrontations.
You must control what others see and hear.
You need other people on your side.
If you are too aggressive, you alienate some people.
If you are too timid, you lose the support of others.
You must offer people a mission that brings them together.

You need the right communication to suit your situation.
You change your methods as the situation changes.
You must expect others to interpret their situation based upon
their position.

5 Warriors maintain a positive attitude.
You can only win confrontations by controlling your emotions.

Conserve your energy before a confrontation.
You must avoid tiring yourself.
Gear up for a confrontation when your opponent wants it least.
Husband your energy.
Opponents fight more adamantly early in the day.
If you wait until later in the day, they will want to back down.
Match your vigor against an opponent's weariness.

[10]Use discipline to await the chaos of battle.
Keep relaxed to await a crisis.
This is how you master emotion.

[13]Stay close to home to await the distant enemy.
Stay comfortable to await the weary enemy.
Stay well fed to await the hungry enemy.
This is how you master power.

Don't entice the enemy when his ranks are orderly.
You must not attack when his formations are solid.
This is how you master adaptation.

[4]You must follow these military rules.
Do not take a position facing the high ground.
Do not oppose those with their backs to the wall.
Do not follow those who pretend to flee.
Do not attack the enemy's strongest men.
Do not swallow the enemy's bait.
Do not block an army that is heading home.
Leave an escape outlet for a surrounded army.
Do not press a desperate foe.
This is how you use military skills.

✦ ✦ ✦

Confrontations take unpredictable turns.
Stay calm when things appear to go wrong.
Match your composure against your opponent's agitation.

Plan confrontations in a place that favors you.
Plan confrontations at a time that favors you.
Plan confrontations when your opponents are out of gas.
This is how you assure a successful showdown.

6 Warriors avoid the mistake of overconfidence.
You must avoid confrontations with well-prepared opponents.
Your success depends only upon your flexibility.

You must let your situation dictate your decisions.
Never fight against a superior position.
Leave your opponents a way to save face.
Avoid the temptation to overextend yourself.
Aim only at your opponents' weaknesses.
See through your opponents' deceptions.
Allow your opponents to back down.
Make it easy for them save face.
Desperation makes opponents more dangerous.
This is the skill of managing confrontations.

Chapter 8

Adaptability: The Mastery of Change

Strategy is a process of continually adjusting to change. Warriors are sensitive to changes in their environment and continually adjust to them. Regular people pay very little attention to what is happening around them and tend to react in the same ways regardless of their situation. In Sun Tzu's view, successful strategy must be dynamic and be based on the willingness to change.

Warriors are masters of change. This chapter serves as an introduction to the next three chapters, which describe a number of specific situations, how to recognize them, and how to respond to them. Regular people have two problems in responding appropriately to the changing situation. Either they fail to recognize opportunities or they fail to take advantage of those opportunities.

Warriors make a habit of change while regular people are unable to change their habits. Though it seems counterintuitive, you must change to be consistent because consistency requires continually adapting to a changing world.

In dealing with change, the best defense is a good offense. If you don't leverage the opportunities of a changing world, others will almost certainly use those changes against you.

The biggest risk in adjusting to change comes from the flaws in your character. Your best qualities can become dangerous when they are taken to extremes. An increased pace of change pressures you toward those extremes.

Adaptability

SUN TZU SAID:

Everyone uses the arts of war. 1
As a general, you get your orders from the government.
You gather your troops.
On dangerous ground, you must not camp.
Where the roads intersect, you must join your allies.
When an area is cut off, you must not delay in it.
When you are surrounded, you must scheme.
In a life-or-death situation, you must fight.
There are roads that you must not take.
There are armies that you must not fight.
There are strongholds that you must not attack.
There are positions that you must not defend.
There are government commands that must not be obeyed.

[14]Military leaders must be experts in knowing how to adapt
to find an advantage.
This will teach you the use of war.

[16]Some commanders are not good at making adjustments to
find an advantage.
They can know the shape of the terrain.
Still, they cannot find an advantageous position.

The Mastery of Change

THE WARRIOR HEARS:

1 Warriors are responsive to their situation.
You always have someone in authority over you.
You always need to assemble resources.
In risky situations, you cannot pretend you are safe.
When the risks are shared, you cannot act like you are alone.
When a path leads nowhere, you must get off it.
When you face overwhelming odds, you can still find an opening.
Fighting is necessary only when you run out of options.
You must know where your decisions lead.
Avoid making the wrong enemies.
Avoid the most difficult battles.
Change your mind rather than defend bad decisions.
Know when doing what you have been told will be a mistake.

Warriors train themselves to recognize their situation so they know the best way to react.
Your good judgment is necessary in competition.

You must make some changes to highlight where your real opportunities are.
You can be very well informed.
Opportunities are hard to find in a static environment.

[19]Some military commanders do not know how to adjust
their methods.
They can find an advantageous position.
Still, they cannot use their men effectively.

You must be creative in your planning. 2
You must adapt to your opportunities and weaknesses.
You can use a variety of approaches and still have a consis-
tent result.
You must adjust to a variety of problems and consistently
solve them.

You can deter your potential enemy by using his 3
weaknesses against him.
You can keep your potential enemy's army busy by giving it
work to do.
You can rush your potential enemy by offering him an
advantageous position.

You must make use of war. 4
Do not trust that the enemy isn't coming.
Trust your readiness to meet him.
Do not trust that the enemy won't attack.
Rely only on your ability to pick a place that the enemy can't
attack.

You cannot keep doing what you have always done and make real progress.
Seeing an opportunity is not enough.
You must change your behavior to take advantage of it.

2 Warriors are not rigid in their planning.
Do more of what works well and less of what isn't working as well.
Consistency comes from constantly improving your position, not from repeating past behavior.
The world changes every day, creating new situations that you cannot ignore.

3 Warriors know how to take the initiative to prevent others from stopping them.
You can leverage a changing situation to more easily create problems for those who oppose you.
You can prevent people from becoming opponents if you can show them other opportunities.

4 Warriors constantly prepare for challenges.
You cannot escape from opposition.
You can only position yourself to overcome it.
You cannot escape from criticism.
You can only protect yourself by taking positions that are easy to defend.

You can exploit five different faults in a leader.
If he is willing to die, you can kill him.
If he wants to survive, you can capture him.
He may have a quick temper.
You can then provoke him with insults.
If he has a delicate sense of honor, you can disgrace him.
If he loves his people, you can create problems for him.
In every situation, look for these five weaknesses.
They are common faults in commanders.
They always lead to military disaster.

[11]To overturn an army, you must kill its general.
To do this, you must use these five weaknesses.
You must always look for them.

5 Warriors know that strengths can turn into weaknesses.
Courage is good, but too much courage is foolhardy.
Caution is good, but too much caution leads to paralysis.
Strategy demands a speedy response.
However, you cannot afford to react emotionally.
Set high standards, but perfectionists are easily frustrated.
Trusting people is good, but dependency is dangerous.
Neither you nor your opponents are perfect.
An opponent's weakness is your opportunity.
Your weakness is an opponent's opportunity.

If you fail, it is because you made poor decisions.
Flaws in your character lead to poor decisions.
Be honest about your weaknesses.

♦ ♦ ♦

Chapter 9

Armed March: The Path of Progress

Success breeds opposition. This chapter teaches the skills you will
need to make progress in the face of opposition. Warriors know
that the key to overcoming opposition is taking the right path.
Taking the right path depends on correctly diagnosing the situation
and choosing the best possible way to react. When you are making
progress, you continually face a variety of situations.

Strategy is situation-based. Sun Tzu categorizes situations by
their unevenness, changing dynamics, and uncertainty. Different
conditions demand different responses. A warrior cannot simply do
as he or she pleases. A warrior only does what the situation requires.
As you move into new areas, you must be aware of your changing
situation, because as your situation changes, you must be prepared
to meet opposition.

Principles and ethics are critical to strong positioning. Competition does not take place in a social vacuum. You need people to support you. Few people are willing to support those without ethics.

The goal is progress, but progress means change. Change creates problems. Change also creates openings for others to attack
you. Warriors are cautious when they are making good progress.

To outmaneuver your opponents, you need to understand what
they are doing. Warriors know that actions speak louder than
words. People never do anything without a purpose. Learning strategy means understanding what motivates people. You want to use
that motivation to rally people to support you.

Armed March

<small>SUN TZU SAID:</small>

Anyone moving an army must adjust to the enemy. 1
When caught in the mountains, rely on their valleys.
Position yourself on the heights facing the sun.
To win your battles, never attack uphill.
This is how you position your army in the mountains.

[6]When water blocks you, keep far away from it.
Let the invader cross the river and wait for him.
Do not meet him in midstream.
Wait for him to get half his forces across and then take
advantage of the situation.

[10]You need to be able to fight.
You can't do that if you are caught in water when you meet
an invader.
Position yourself upstream, facing the sun.
Never face against the current.
Always position your army upstream when near the water.

The Path of Progress

THE WARRIOR HEARS:

1 Warriors make progress by outmaneuvering their opponents.
When the playing field is uneven, follow the path of least resistance.
Strategy requires that you use the unevenness of the ground.
You never meet opponents when they control the high ground.
You can make progress by using the inequities of the ground.

When change becomes an obstacle, you must be cautious.
When others are tempted into difficult transitions, be patient.
You should never join them.
You want to meet your opponents after their transitions have weakened and divided them.

You must overcome opponents.
You cannot fight the trends and deal with your opponents at the same time.
You must use the pressure of change in your favor.
Use the trends instead of fighting them.
Your progress depends on getting the forces of change on your side.

¹⁵You may have to move across marshes.
Move through them quickly without stopping.
You may meet the enemy in the middle of a marsh.
You must keep on the water grasses.
Keep your back to a clump of trees.
This is how you position your army in a marsh.

²¹On a level plateau, take a position that you can change.
Keep the higher ground on your right and to the rear.
Keep danger in front of you and safety behind.
This is how you position yourself on a level plateau.

²⁵You can find an advantage in all four of these situations.
Learn from the great emperor who used positioning to conquer his four rivals.

Armies are stronger on high ground and weaker on low. 2
They are better camping on sunny southern hillsides than on shady northern ones.
Provide for your army's health and place men correctly.
Your army will be free from disease.
Done correctly, this means victory.

⁶You must sometimes defend on a hill or riverbank.
You must keep on the south side in the sun.
Keep the uphill slope at your right rear.

⁹This will give the advantage to your army.
It will always give you a position of strength.

Sometimes you must get through an uncertain situation.
You must get through these times without getting bogged down.
Enemies can move against you when your situation is unclear.
All you can do is stick to what you know.
You must avoid getting pushed into a worse mess.
You must make progress even when your situation is unclear.

When all things are equal, you want to keep your options open.
You must use every advantage of your position.
Face your opponents directly but keep a fallback position.
You can make good progress on an equal playing field.

You can find opportunities in every situation you face.
Warriors master the techniques necessary to overcome opponents
under any conditions.

2 Warriors know how to recognize the ethical high ground.
People are more vigorous working out in the open than they are
working secretly.
Principled, honorable positions strengthen your support.
Corrupt, dishonest positions make people cynical.
Ethical behavior translates to long-term success.

Sometimes you are forced to defend a questionable position.
You can still be honest about your situation.
You need strong support behind you.

Strong principles create opportunities.
Principles also create unity, which is the source of strength.

Stop the march when the rain swells the river into rapids. 3
You may want to ford the river.
Wait until it subsides.

4All regions can have seasonal mountain streams that can
cut you off.
There are seasonal lakes.
There are seasonal blockages.
There are seasonal jungles.
There are seasonal floods.
There are seasonal fissures.
Get away from all these quickly.
Do not get close to them.
Keep them at a distance.
Maneuver the enemy close to them.
Position yourself facing these dangers.
Push the enemy back into them.

16Danger can hide on your army's flank.
There are reservoirs and lakes.
There are reeds and thickets.
There are mountain woods.
Their dense vegetation provides a hiding place.
You must cautiously search through them.
They can always hide an ambush.

3 Warriors never let themselves become overwhelmed by change.
You must navigate change.
This requires patience.

The changing climate is continually reshaping your situation, creating obstacles.
You can drown in temporary obstacles.
Others will simply stop you.
Others are just confusing.
Some can be suddenly overwhelming.
Then there are bottomless pits.
You use speed to go around obstacles.
The sooner you react the better.
It is always quicker to avoid obstacles than to deal with them.
Use your opponents' ignorance of obstacles against them.
A rival's first instinct is to oppose you.
You can use this reaction to pin him or her against obstacles.

Not all dangers are readily apparent.
There are dangers in change.
There are dangers in growth.
There are dangers in growing inequity.
You have to be wary of hidden threats.
Trust your suspicions.
You cannot afford to be blindsided.

Sometimes, the enemy is close by but remains calm. 4
Expect to find him in a natural stronghold.
Other times he remains at a distance but provokes battle.
He wants you to attack him.

5He sometimes shifts the position of his camp.
He is looking for an advantageous position.

7The trees in the forest move.
Expect that the enemy is coming.
The tall grasses obstruct your view.
Be suspicious.

11The birds take flight.
Expect that the enemy is hiding.
Animals startle.
Expect an ambush.

15Notice the dust.
It sometimes rises high in a straight line.
Vehicles are coming.
The dust appears low in a wide band.
Foot soldiers are coming.
The dust seems scattered in different areas.
The enemy is collecting firewood.
Any dust is light and settling down.
The enemy is setting up camp.

4 Warriors know how to interpret the actions of others.
When people are confident, they have a secret advantage.
Even those far away can still act in a threatening manner.
They don't invite attack without a reason.

People do not normally move from where they are comfortable.
They move only to pursue opportunities.

Observe the people around you for unexplained changes.
These changes indicate that someone is up to something.
You have to be wary when you can't see what opponents are doing.
You cannot be too careful.

Sensitive people sense changes first.
They can alert you to what is happening behind the scenes.
People can appear nervous.
This can mean an attack is coming.

Every action leaves some small sign.
These signs can be obvious and point in the same direction.
This indicates others moving very quickly.
Signs can be subtle and broad.
This indicates others moving very broadly.
Signs can pop up here and there.
This indicates others slowing down.
Signs can be spotty and declining.
This indicates others pausing.

Your enemy speaks humbly while building up forces. 5
He is planning to advance.

³The enemy talks aggressively and pushes as if to advance.
He is planning to retreat.

⁵Small vehicles exit his camp first.
They move the army's flanks.
They are forming a battle line.

⁸Your enemy tries to sue for peace but without offering a
treaty.
He is plotting.

¹⁰Your enemy's men run to leave and yet form ranks.
You should expect action.

¹²Half his army advances and the other half retreats.
He is luring you.

¹⁴Your enemy plans to fight but his men just stand there.
They are starving.

¹⁶Those who draw water drink it first.
They are thirsty.

¹⁸Your enemy sees an advantage but does not advance.
His men are tired.

5 Warriors notice when people's words differ from their actions.
An opponent is trying to mislead you.

You need not fear the most aggressive behavior.
It is often a smoke screen for weakness.

Notice when people suddenly change in subtle ways.
Notice when they defend themselves too quickly.
They want to pick a fight.

Anyone can say that they want peace, but they are not serious if
they reject compromises that permit peace.
Peace can be just a trick.

When people are afraid of you, they befriend each other.
They can unite against you.

Distrust obvious weakness on the part of your opponents.
They may be tempting you to act rashly.

When a rival's supporters do nothing, there is always a reason.
They lack resources.

Individuals in groups can act in their personal self-interest.
They no longer trust their organization.

Your opponents may fail to seize an obvious opportunity.
Their resources are exhausted.

²⁰Birds gather.
Your enemy has abandoned his camp.

²²Your enemy's soldiers call in the night.
They are afraid.

²⁴Your enemy's army is raucous.
The men do not take their commander seriously.

²⁶Your enemy's banners and flags shift.
Order is breaking down.

²⁸Your enemy's officers are irritable.
They are exhausted.

³⁰Your enemy's men kill their horses for meat.
They are out of provisions.

³²They don't put their pots away or return to their tents.
They are desperate.

³⁴Enemy troops appear sincere and agreeable.
But their men are slow to speak to each other.
They are no longer united.

³⁷Your enemy offers too many incentives to his men.
He is in trouble.

³⁹Your enemy gives out too many punishments.
His men are weary.

Scavengers can be informative.
When people move on, scavengers follow behind.

A group of people shows their emotions.
Their fear is contagious.

Any group can react wildly.
It means the members have lost confidence in their leader.

Reorganization is another sign of weakness.
It indicates a breakdown of unity and focus.

Poor decisions are made in anger.
Weariness is the source of most anger.

Only desperate people sacrifice their mobility.
Only survival is more important.

Some people are indifferent to self-preservation.
These people are dangerous.

Communication is the key to coordination.
Friends can be reluctant to share information.
Their friendship is weak.

People shouldn't have to bribe their supporters.
This is a sign of discord.

People also shouldn't punish their supporters.
This is a sign of laziness.

⁴¹Your enemy first acts violently and then is afraid of your
larger force.
His best troops have not arrived.

⁴³Your enemy comes in a conciliatory manner.
He needs to rest and recuperate.

⁴⁵Your enemy is angry and appears to welcome battle.
This goes on for a long time, but he doesn't attack.
He also doesn't leave the field.
You must watch him carefully.

If you are too weak to fight, you must find more men. 6
In this situation, you must not act aggressively.
You must unite your forces.
Prepare for the enemy.
Recruit men and stay where you are.

⁶You must be cautious about making plans and adjust to the
enemy.
You must gather more men.

Opponents can attack before they are ready, to throw us off balance and delay our progress.
They may expect additional support soon.

Opponents can suddenly pretend that they to want to be friends.
This can also be a delaying tactic.

Sometimes your rivals' behavior is just confusing.
They don't know if they want to confront you or not.
They won't leave you alone.
Your vigilance is your best defense against them.

6 When your progress stalls, you need more resources.
You must not challenge your opposition.
You must gather your resources.
Prepare to defend yourself.
Build up support where you are.

Plan on defending yourself and keep track of what opponents are doing.
You must buy time to build up your resources.

With new, undedicated soldiers, you can depend on them 7
if you discipline them.
They will tend to disobey your orders.
If they do not obey your orders, they will be useless.

4You can depend on seasoned, dedicated soldiers.
But you must avoid disciplining them without reason.
Otherwise, you cannot use them.

7You must control your soldiers with esprit de corps.
You must bring them together by winning victories.
You must get them to believe in you.

10Make it easy for people to know what to do by training
your people.
Your people will then obey you.
If you do not make it easy for people to know what to do,
you won't train your people.
Then they will not obey.

14Make your commands easy to follow.
You must understand the way a crowd thinks.

7 Warriors use discipline because they must train their apprentices to be dependable.
Novices lack good judgment.
To be productive, you begin by following orders.

When you develop experience, you become dependable.
You need neither direction nor punishment to do what is needed.
This makes you valuable.

All teams must have an identity that they share.
When people share successes, their friendships are solidified.
Trust is the foundation of all teams.

You train other people by making it easy for other people to know what to do and why.
This is the key to leadership.
If you send mixed messages about what is needed and why, others cannot know how to act.
They also lose faith in you.

Keep all instructions straightforward and simple.
Know how people are likely to interpret what you are saying.

Chapter 10

地 形

Field Position: The Vision of Opportunity

Everyone holds a number of different positions in life. At school, at work, and even in our personal lives, our roles are always changing. Warriors think of every position that they hold as a stepping-stone to future success. Each role in life represents a special type of opportunity. Each position has its own advantages and disadvantages. Your current role and abilities reveal your next opportunity.

Not all positions are the same. Warriors know how to make the right moves so that each step makes the step after that easier. Strategy provides a simple method for weighing your opportunities so you can make the right choices. After awhile, you will instantly see where each choice will naturally lead.

The vision you follow is largely a matter of your character. Warriors are sensitive to the personal flaws that handicap regular people. Warriors work to eliminate these flaws in themselves while they work to exploit these flaws in others.

Warriors do not make choices to satisfy other people's expectations. You are the only person in a position to choose the right course for you. Warriors do not make their choices based upon a desire to win praise or avoid criticism.

Warriors recognize their responsibility to their loved ones. They recognize that they must act as leaders and role models. Giving people what they need is more important than giving them what they want. To choose the right path in life is a matter of being objective about your obstacles, capabilities, and principles.

Field Position

Some field positions are unobstructed. 1
Some field positions are entangling.
Some field positions are supporting.
Some field positions are constricted.
Some field positions give you a barricade.
Some field positions are spread out.

7You can attack from some positions easily.
Other forces can meet you easily as well.
We call these unobstructed positions.
These positions are open.
On them, be the first to occupy a high, sunny area.
Put yourself where you can defend your supply routes.
Then you will have an advantage.

The Vision of Opportunity

1 Warriors recognize when their roles are wide open.
They recognize roles that cannot be recaptured.
They recognize roles that last a lifetime.
They recognize roles that are controlling.
They recognize roles that protect them.
They recognize roles that are too diluted.

Some roles offer you a variety of ways to move forward.
Your rivals can easily challenge any of your moves.
These roles are wide open opportunities.
They are open to you and to your opponents as well.
You must use speed to get the benefit of them as stepping-stones.
As you move forward, consider your long-term needs.
These roles offer the easiest path to the future.

¹⁴You can attack from some positions easily.

Disaster arises when you try to return to them.

These are entangling positions.

These field positions are one-sided.

Wait until your enemy is unprepared.

You can then attack from these positions and win.

Avoid a well-prepared enemy.

You will try to attack and lose.

Since you can't return, you will meet disaster.

These field positions offer no advantage.

²⁴You cannot leave some positions without losing an advantage.

If the enemy leaves this ground, he also loses an advantage.

We call these supporting field positions.

These positions strengthen you.

The enemy may try to entice you away.

Still, hold your position.

You must entice the enemy to leave.

You then strike him as he is leaving.

These field positions offer an advantage.

³³Some field positions are constricted.

Get to these positions first.

You must fill these areas and await the enemy.

Sometimes, the enemy will reach them first.

If he fills them, do not follow him.

However, if he fails to fill them, you can go after him.

Some roles offer you opportunities, but with a catch.

If you abandon these roles, they are gone forever.

You cannot return to them.

They are like a one-way street.

You must be patient to use these roles as stepping-stones.

You must be certain your next opportunity is solid.

You cannot make the wrong move.

Do not move out of these roles unless you are certain.

These roles offer you no fallback position.

These roles are not the most beneficial.

Some roles are perfect opportunities that no similar position can improve upon.

No one who attains these positions can afford to leave them.

You want these roles to last a lifetime.

The advantage they offer never diminishes.

Everyone will try to tempt you out of these roles.

You must appreciate how rare these situations are.

Let other people take them for granted.

When others abandon these roles, move instantly.

These positions are well worth controlling.

Some roles are exclusive.

The first person to win them can take control.

If you attain these positions first, you can stop rivals behind you.

If other people reach these positions first, observe how they behave.

If they bar your progress, do not challenge them.

If they do not block you, you can follow behind them.

³⁹Some field positions give you a barricade.
Get to these positions first.
You must occupy their southern, sunny heights in order to
await the enemy.
Sometimes the enemy occupies these areas first.
If so, entice him away.
Never go after him.

⁴⁵Some field positions are too spread out.
Your force may seem equal to the enemy.
Still you will lose if you provoke a battle.
If you fight, you will not have any advantage.

⁴⁹These are the six types of field positions.
Each battleground has its own rules.
As a commander, you must know where to go.
You must examine each position closely.

Some armies can be outmaneuvered. 2
Some armies are too lax.
Some armies fall down.
Some armies fall apart.
Some armies are disorganized.
Some armies must retreat.

⁷Know all six of these weaknesses.
They create weak timing and disastrous positions.
They all arise from the army's commander.

Some roles can protect you.

You want to get into these roles quickly.

These roles give you authority and visibility that is easy to use if you are patient.

You must recognize when your opponents are in these roles.

Your rivals are protected by these roles.

You cannot attack them directly.

Some roles are too diluted.

These positions undermine your strength.

When you fall into these roles, you are weak compared with others.

These roles make it difficult to meet a challenge.

You must recognize the abstract forms of these six roles.

Every real role combines their qualities to some degree.

As a warrior, you have a choice about what roles you play.

You must understand the underlying nature of your opportunity.

2 Warriors recognize confusion.

They recognize laziness.

They recognize a lack of training.

They recognize insecurity.

They recognize self-indulgence.

They recognize a lack of foresight.

You must recognize these weaknesses in yourself and in others.

These weaknesses make progress impossible past a certain point.

They are simply character flaws.

[10]One general can command a force equal to the enemy.
Still his enemy outflanks him.
This means that his army can be outmaneuvered.

[13]Another can have strong soldiers but weak officers.
This means that his army is too lax.

[15]Another has strong officers but weak soldiers.
This means that his army will fall down.

[17]Another has subcommanders who are angry and defiant.
They attack the enemy and fight their own battles.
The commander cannot know the battlefield.
This means that his army will fall apart.

[21]Another general is weak and easygoing.
He fails to make his orders clear.
His officers and men lack direction.
This shows in his military formations.
This means that his army is disorganized.

[26]Another general fails to predict the enemy.
He pits his small forces against larger ones.
His weak forces attack stronger ones.
He fails to pick his fights correctly.
This means that his army must retreat.

Some people start with every advantage in life.
Still, others consistently outperform them.
These people are confused.

Some people have good skills but lack drive.
These people are too lazy.

Some people have drive but lack good skills.
These people are untrained.

Some people are easily upset and confrontational.
They attack others and are always defending themselves.
They lose track of what their goals are.
These people are insecure.

Some people are indecisive and carefree.
They never identify their goals.
Their drive and skills lack any focus.
They take new positions on any whim.
These people are self-indulgent.

Some people never think about their future.
They invest too little effort into pursuing long-term gains.
They spend more than they earn.
They are always coming up short.
These people are short-sighted.

³¹You must know all about these six weaknesses.
You must understand the philosophies that lead to defeat.
When a general arrives, you can know what he will do.
You must study each general carefully.

You must control your field position. 3
It will always strengthen your army.

³You must predict the enemy to overpower him and win.
You must analyze the obstacles, dangers, and distances.
This is the best way to command.

⁶Understand your field position before you go to battle.
Then you will win.
You can fail to understand your field position and still fight.
Then you will lose.

¹⁰You must provoke battle when you will certainly win.
It doesn't matter what you are ordered.
The government may order you not to fight.
Despite that, you must always fight when you will win.

¹⁴Sometimes provoking a battle will lead to a loss.
The government may order you to fight.
Despite that, you must avoid battle when you will lose.

You must instantly see through these character flaws.
Certain worldviews lead to these weaknesses.
People with these flaws are very predictable.
You must analyze yourself and others.

3 A warrior uses every opportunity as a stepping-stone.
Each step must improve your position.

You must foresee how you can meet opposition and still succeed.
Choose your path by considering the problems it might lead to.
Everything depends on making the right decisions.

You must examine your options before you accept any challenge.
You will naturally choose the easiest path.
Unfortunately, most people seldom look before they leap.
This is why they so often fail.

You must accept every challenge that leads to success.
You do not need to do what everyone expects.
Regular people are controlled by the expectations of others.
Warriors are dedicated to constant progress toward better positions.

You must avoid every challenge that leads to failure.
Do not let others pressure you into undertaking them.
You cannot waste your time on paths that take you nowhere.

[17]You must advance without desiring praise.
You must retreat without fearing shame.
The only correct move is to preserve your troops.
This is how you serve your country.
This is how you reward your nation.

Think of your soldiers as little children. 4
You can make them follow you into a deep river.
Treat them as your beloved children.
You can lead them all to their deaths.

[5]Some leaders are generous but cannot use their men.
They love their men but cannot command them.
Their men are unruly and disorganized.
These leaders create spoiled children.
Their soldiers are useless.

You may know what your soldiers will do in an attack. 5
You may not know if the enemy is vulnerable to attack.
You will then win only half the time.
You may know that the enemy is vulnerable to attack.
You may not know if your men have the capability of attack-
ing him.
You will still win only half the time.
You may know that the enemy is vulnerable to attack.
You may know that your men are ready to attack.
You may not, however, know how to position yourself in the
field for battle.
You will still win only half the time.

You must put aside your desire for praise.

You must put aside your fear of failure.

You must use your limited resources in the best possible way.

This is the only way you really satisfy others.

This is how you do your duty.

4 Warriors recognize their influence over friends and family.

You must take responsibility for the people you love.

You must accept your responsibility.

You must recognize your power to affect their lives.

Regular people think they should give everyone what they want.

They supply affection when people really need direction.

This makes people unhappy and confused.

Pampering people destroys their ability to make decisions.

This results in tragedy.

5 Warriors know exactly how their abilities help them advance.

Regular people forget to think about the obstacles in their path.

This is why failure is so common.

You can know exactly how to overcome the obstacles in your path.

You still must have the abilities and resources needed to meet those challenges at hand.

Without preparation, success is a coin flip.

You can know exactly how to overcome the obstacles in your path.

You can have the abilities and resources to meet those challenges.

You must also know how to select each opportunity as a stepping-stone to future success.

You do not want to fail because you chose the wrong path.

[11]You must know how to make war.
You can then act without confusion.
You can attempt anything.

[14]We say:
Know the enemy and know yourself.
Your victory will be painless.
Know the weather and the field.
Your victory will be complete.

✦ ✦ ✦

You must see your path clearly.
You work toward success one step at a time.
No eventual goal is too large.

Warriors know the truth.
You match your skills to the obstacles before you.
Success will come easily.
Use the trends and your opportunities.
There is no limit to your success.

Chapter 11

九地

Types of Terrain: The Miracle of Training

Becoming a warrior requires developing a warrior's mind. The warrior's mind is trained in perception and decision-making. The warrior's mind sees the key relationships that define a situation and reacts instantly based on training.

To know how to respond, you don't have to know how to sort through thousands, hundreds, or even dozens of different situations. Sun Tzu defines only nine basic situations that require a specific form of response. Warriors can act instantly and confidently based on their recognition of these situations.

Strategy is a process of continually leveraging your opportunities. You must always expand your capabilities. When you commit yourself to continual progress, you must also commit yourself to refining your decision-making skills.

When you are confident in your decisions, you are committed to a course of action. Warriors appreciate the power of commitment. When you are truly committed, you no longer waste your efforts preparing for failure. After a commitment is made, the most important quality is your speed of response. A warrior's responses are a trained reflex.

Trained decision-makers are natural leaders. You can accomplish little alone. You need the support of others to be successful. Good leadership requires identifying the best challenges to tackle. New challenges hold a team together and keep it moving forward.

Types of Terrain

SUN TZU SAID:

Use the art of war. 1
Know when the terrain will scatter you.
Know when the terrain will be easy.
Know when the terrain will be disputed.
Know when the terrain is open.
Know when the terrain is intersecting.
Know when the terrain is dangerous.
Know when the terrain is bad.
Know when the terrain is confined.
Know when the terrain is deadly.

¹¹Warring parties must sometimes fight inside their own
territory.
This is scattering terrain.

¹³When you enter hostile territory, your penetration is shallow.
This is easy terrain.

¹⁵Some terrain gives you an advantageous position.
But it gives others an advantageous position as well.
This will be disputed terrain.

The Miracle of Training

1 Warriors act on training.
You must recognize circumstances that divide people.
You must recognize simple challenges.
You must recognize sources of conflict.
You must recognize when you have few obstacles.
You must recognize when circumstances bring people together.
You must recognize difficult challenges.
You must recognize when progress will be difficult.
You must recognize when you are vulnerable.
You must recognize when you are desperate.

Learn what happens when people are threatened where they once felt safe.
Their unity dissolves.

Learn to expect a honeymoon period in a new project or campaign.
Your progress seems so simple.

Learn that areas that are too desirable create conflict.
If you want to win these rewards, so will many others.
These situations are sources of conflict.

[18]You can use some terrain to advance easily.
Others can advance along with you.
This is open terrain.

[21]Everyone shares access to a given area.
The first one to arrive there can gather a larger group than
anyone else.
This is intersecting terrain.

[24]You can penetrate deeply into hostile territory.
Then many hostile cities are behind you.
This is dangerous terrain.

[27]There are mountain forests.
There are dangerous obstructions.
There are reservoirs.
Everyone confronts these obstacles on a campaign.
They make bad terrain.

[32]In some areas, the entry passage is narrow.
You are closed in as you try to get out of them.
In this type of area, a few people can effectively attack your
much larger force.
This is confined terrain.

[36]You can sometimes survive only if you fight quickly.
You will die if you delay.
This is deadly terrain.

Learn what happens when you are making quick progress.
Everyone else is probably making good progress as well.
These situations have few real obstacles.

Learn about areas in which people's interests naturally come together.
Use these areas to aggressively build a team and organize team-mates for a shared goal.
Use the circumstances to bring people together.

Learn that a project or campaign changes as time goes on.
The more progress you make, the more resistance you encounter.
These challenges are increasingly difficult.

Learn when you must work your way through problems.
You must be very careful of some situations.
You must work your way around some obstacles.
You never make progress without encountering problems.
These situations slow down your progress.

Learn to recognize critical transition points.
These situations limit what you can do.
You are dependent on others and defenseless against attack in these situations.
Critical transitions make you vulnerable.

Learn when you must react instantly to a challenge.
Wasting even a minute can be fatal.
You are truly desperate.

³⁹To be successful, you must control scattering terrain by avoiding battle.

Control easy terrain by not stopping.

Control disputed terrain by not attacking.

Control open terrain by staying with the enemy's forces.

Control intersecting terrain by uniting with your allies.

Control dangerous terrain by plundering.

Control bad terrain by keeping on the move.

Control confined terrain by using surprise.

Control deadly terrain by fighting.

Go to an area that is known to be good for waging war. 2

Use it to cut off the enemy's contact between his front and back lines.

Prevent his small parties from relying on his larger force.

Stop his strong divisions from rescuing his weak ones.

Prevent his officers from getting their men together.

Chase his soldiers apart to stop them from amassing.

Harass them to prevent their ranks from forming.

⁸When joining battle gives you an advantage, you must do it.

When it isn't to your benefit, you must avoid it.

¹⁰A daring soldier may ask:

"A large, organized enemy army and its general are coming.

What do I do to prepare for them?"

Since a challenge in your own area is divisive, success depends on moving into new areas.

Success depends on getting the most out of your initial progress.

Success depends on avoiding prizes everyone is fighting for.

Success depends on speed when there are few obstacles.

Success depends on finding opportunities to build alliances.

Success depends on getting rewarded for expensive projects.

Success depends on working through every obstacle.

Success depends on keeping your vulnerabilities a secret.

Success depends on fighting only when you are desperate.

2 Warriors train to identify situations that offer opportunities. These situations offer you an opening that allows you to divide and conquer.

You can win small victories in the face of serious challenges.

You can avoid serious opposition while solving minor problems.

You stop little problems from becoming more serious.

You make quick progress to prevent opposition from growing.

Your progress makes it difficult for critics to attack you.

When meeting a challenge creates such opportunities, meet it.

When a challenge offers you no such opportunities, avoid it.

Warriors need training.

It is sometimes obvious when you are going to be attacked.

You must know how to defend yourself.

¹³Tell him:

"First seize an area that the enemy must have.

Then he will pay attention to you.

Mastering speed is the essence of war.

Take advantage of a large enemy's inability to keep up.

Use a philosophy of avoiding difficult situations.

Attack the area where he doesn't expect you."

You must use the philosophy of an invader. 3

Invade deeply and then concentrate your forces.

This controls your men without oppressing them.

⁴Get your supplies from the riches of the territory.

They are sufficient to supply your whole army.

⁶Take care of your men and do not overtax them.

Your esprit de corps increases your momentum.

Keep your army moving and plan for surprises.

Make it difficult for the enemy to count your forces.

Position your men where there is no place to run.

They will then face death without fleeing.

They will find a way to survive.

Your officers and men will fight to their utmost.

¹⁴Military officers who are committed lose their fear.

When they have nowhere to run, they must stand firm.

Deep in enemy territory, they are captives.

Since they cannot escape, they will fight.

Your reaction is simple.
Instead of defending yourself, look for your opponent's weakness.
By targeting a weakness, you shift your opponent's focus.
Speed is important because it gives you the initiative.
If you maintain the initiative, opponents don't know where to turn.
You avoid fighting in your own territory, even to defend yourself.
You must move the battle where your opponent doesn't want it.

3 Warriors are trained to use the power of commitment.
When people are deeply committed, they develop better focus.
Commitment maintains a team's focus without creating divisions.

Being committed to conquering a new area is always rewarding.
New challenges stimulate everyone.

Take care of your teammates and don't push them too hard.
Nurture a sense of team spirit to keep everyone united.
You maintain your momentum by preparing for things to go wrong.
You want your opponents to underestimate you.
You want solid commitments from your teammates.
Once people are committed, they cannot back down.
You will learn what you need to do to succeed.
Working together gets the best efforts out of everyone.

When you make a commitment, your uncertainty vanishes.
Once you choose a course of action, you must stay with it.
The more opposition you overcome, the stronger you become.
You must not leave yourself an easy way to back out.

18Commit your men completely.
Without being posted, they will be on guard.
Without being asked, they will get what is needed.
Without being forced, they will be dedicated.
Without being given orders, they can be trusted.

23Stop them from guessing by removing all their doubts.
Stop them from dying by giving them no place to run.

25Your officers may not be rich.
Nevertheless, they still desire plunder.
They may die young.
Nevertheless, they still want to live forever.

29You must order the time of attack.
Officers and men may sit and weep until their lapels are wet.
When they stand up, tears may stream down their cheeks.
Put them in a position where they cannot run.
They will show the greatest courage under fire.

Make good use of war. 4
This demands instant reflexes.
You must develop these instant reflexes.
Act like an ordinary mountain snake.
If people strike your head then stop them with your tail.
If they strike your tail then stop them with your head.
If they strike your middle then use both your head and tail.

Choose teammates who are devoted.

You want them to share your sense of responsibility.

Their judgment can be as valuable as your own.

People shouldn't have to be nagged to do what is needed.

You must be able to trust your teammates' devotion.

You must stop second-guessing yourself to be confident.

Your success is more certain when you stop looking for excuses.

People are motivated by self-interest.

Everyone wants greater success.

People are willing to take risks.

This doesn't mean that they don't value what they have.

The time comes when everyone must act.

People will argue and complain until that time comes.

Even when the time comes, they will still complain.

Once people make a commitment, they cannot back down.

People show incredible courage when they commit themselves.

4 Warriors train to react quickly.

You must know how to instantly respond to any situation.

Train yourself to recognize these nine situations.

Your responses should be instinctual.

Every member of your team must know how to react.

You must be able to make your decisions instantly.

You and your teammates must know how defend yourselves.

[8]A daring soldier asks:
"Can any army imitate these instant reflexes?"
We answer:
"It can."

[12]To command and get the most out of proud people, you
must study adversity.
People work together when they are in the same boat during
a storm.
In this situation, one rescues the other just as the right
hand helps the left.

[15]Use adversity correctly.
Tether your horses and bury your wagon's wheels.
Still, you can't depend on this alone.
An organized force is braver than lone individuals.
This is the art of organization.
Put the tough and weak together.
You must also use the terrain.

[22]Make good use of war.
Unite your men as one.
Never let them give up.

The commander must be a military professional. 5
This requires confidence and detachment.
You must maintain dignity and order.
You must control what your men see and hear.
They must follow you without knowing your plans.

Is speed always possible?
Can a group of people always know how to work together?
Your training is the key.
You must train as a team.

Sharing a common enemy and common dangers draws people together.
The more teammates have to lose, the most smoothly they work together.
When the threat is big enough, people don't think twice about helping one another.

A threatening situation can work for you.
You can tell yourself that you are totally committed to your course.
Your individual commitment alone will not save you.
When others are depending on you, you forget your personal fears.
This the real power of teamwork.
The range of a team's abilities overcomes its flaws.
You must use your situation.

Strategy is the key to success.
Unity is the source of strength.
Persistence assures your success.

5 Warriors train in the art of leadership.
You must demonstrate self-assurance and objectivity.
Teammates must respect your seriousness and your priorities.
Always pay attention to the impression you are creating.
People must have faith in the decisions that you make.

⁶You can reinvent your men's roles.

You can change your plans.

You can use your men without their understanding.

⁹You must shift your campgrounds.

You must take detours from the ordinary routes.

You must use men without telling them about your strategy.

¹²A commander provides what is needed now.

This is like climbing high and being willing to kick away your ladder.

You must be able to lead your men deep into different surrounding territory.

And yet, you can discover the opportunity to win.

¹⁶You must drive men like a flock of sheep.

You must drive them to march.

You must drive them to attack.

You must never let them know where you are headed.

You must unite them into a great army.

You must then drive them against all opposition.

This is the job of a true commander.

²³You must adapt to the different terrain.

You must adapt to find an advantage.

You must manage your people's affections.

You must study all these skills.

You must see the possibilities in everyone.

Your goals must always evolve.

You can get more out of people than they know they have to give.

You can break teammates of their old habits.

You can lead them to places they never expected to go.

They can accept your decisions without debating them.

Focus on getting others to join you in taking the next step.

You ratchet up huge commitment one step at a time, leaving others no way to back down.

You prove your leadership by moving people out of their comfort zone and by opening up new possibilities.

This is how teamwork creates such tremendous successes.

It is always your responsibility to guide people.

You must keep them moving forward.

You must keep them exploring new areas.

You must avoid setting limits on your goals.

The unity of the team is the source of its power.

The power of teamwork overcomes any obstacle.

If you want to be a warrior, you must be a leader.

Adjust your techniques to fit your situation.

Every situation is full of opportunities if you are open to them.

You can get people to care about what must be done.

Train yourself to inspire others.

Always use the philosophy of invasion. 6
Deep invasions concentrate your forces.
Shallow invasions scatter your forces.
When you leave your country and cross the border, you must
take control.
This is always critical ground.
You can sometimes move in any direction.
This is always intersecting ground.
You can penetrate deeply into a territory.
This is always dangerous ground.
You penetrate only a little way.
This is always easy ground.
Your retreat is closed and the path ahead tight.
This is always confined ground.
There is sometimes no place to run.
This is always deadly ground.

[16]To use scattering terrain correctly, you must inspire your
men's devotion.
On easy terrain, you must keep in close communication.
On disputed terrain, you try to hamper the enemy's progress.
On open terrain, you must carefully defend your chosen position.
On intersecting terrain, you must solidify your alliances.
On dangerous terrain, you must ensure your food supplies.
On bad terrain, you must keep advancing along the road.
On confined terrain, you must stop information leaks from
your headquarters.
On deadly terrain, you must show what you can do by
killing the enemy.

6 Warriors train to expand their possibilities.
The bigger the challenge, the more inspiring it is.
Defending existing positions has a tendency to divide people.
When you move into new areas, you must make a serious commitment to keep going.
This initial commitment is vital.
Even when you are committed, you still have options.
Choose options that unite you with your teammates.
You can invest only so much into a specific direction.
The direction you choose must pay off.
At the beginning, progress is relatively painless.
You want to make movement as easy as possible.
You must cross certain bridges when you come to them.
Keep these critical transitions a secret.
You can run out of options.
Fight when your future depends on it.

When you must defend your own territory, focus on shared values to maintain unity.
You must remind teammates not to take easy progress for granted.
Go after contested prizes only when you have an edge.
Know when no obstacles prevent opponents from turning on you.
Friendships are forged from shared opportunities.
The bigger the task, the more certain you must be of your resources.
When the going gets tough, look for the best way to get through it.
You must keep your vulnerabilities a secret, especially from those who can control you.
The only way to show your desperation is by making your opponents look bad.

²⁵Make your men feel like an army.
Surround them and they will defend themselves.
If they cannot avoid it, they will fight.
If they are under pressure, they will obey.

Do the right thing when you don't know your 7
different enemies' plans.
Don't attempt to meet them.

³You don't know the position of mountain forests, dangerous
obstructions, and reservoirs?
Then you cannot march the army.
You don't have local guides?
You won't get any of the benefits of the terrain.

⁷There are many factors in war.
You may lack knowledge of any one of them.
If so, it is wrong to take a nation into war.

¹⁰You must be able to control your government's war.
If you divide a big nation, it will be unable to put together a
large force.
Increase your enemy's fear of your ability.
Prevent his forces from getting together and organizing.

Each member adds value to your team.

Put teammates in situations in which they must do their best.

Deny teammates the temptation of a good excuse.

Use the situation to win commitment.

7 Warriors are trained to know that they cannot advance where they cannot see.

Avoid acting out of ignorance.

You cannot let yourself be surprised by every problem, obstacle, and opponent you encounter.

You need knowledge to choose the right path.

There is no replacement for experience.

Only training teaches you how to use your position.

You need a framework for understanding your situation.

The goal of training is to make your blind spots obvious.

Only fools endanger themselves through ignorance.

You must earn the trust of people in authority over you.

Divide every goal and problem into small tasks that you can complete one at a time.

You should not fear others; they should fear you.

You must undermine and divide any potential opposition.

¹⁴Do the right thing and do not arrange outside alliances
before their time.
You will not have to assert your authority prematurely.
Trust only yourself and your self-interest.
This increases the enemy's fear of you.
You can make one of his allies withdraw.
His whole nation can fall.

²⁰Distribute rewards without worrying about having a system.
Halt without the government's command.
Attack with the whole strength of your army.
Use your army as if it were a single man.

²⁴Attack with skill.
Do not discuss it.
Attack when you have an advantage.
Do not talk about the dangers.
When you can launch your army into deadly ground, even if
it stumbles, it can still survive.
You can be weakened in a deadly battle and yet be stronger
afterward.

³⁰Even a large force can fall into misfortune.
If you fall behind, however, you can still turn defeat into victory.
You must use the skills of war.
To survive, you must adapt yourself to your enemy's purpose.
You must stay with him no matter where he goes.
It may take a thousand miles to kill the general.
If you correctly understand him, you can find the skill to do it.

Alliances can be extremely useful, but they can also limit many of your options.

Disagreements about direction can slow down your progress.

You must know exactly what you want out of an alliance.

Your certainty increases your rivals' uncertainty.

Your confidence can win over a rival's allies.

It can destroy a rival's credibility.

Use your own judgment about who deserves the fruits of success.

No one can force you into an opportunity.

Go forward only when you are completely committed to success.

When everyone supports a move, your success is assured.

Move forward carefully.

Bragging about future success is foolish.

Move forward when an opportunity presents itself.

Worrying about possible failure is worthless.

You will get another chance even when you take needless risks and make avoidable mistakes.

You will learn a painful but memorable lesson from picking the wrong battles.

Even when the odds are in your favor, tragedy can strike.

There are opportunities hidden in even the most painful setbacks.

You must see how your situation has changed.

After a disaster, you must learn from your opponents' philosophy.

You must measure yourself against your opponents.

You must do whatever it takes to surpass your rivals.

If you learn what they know, you can eventually succeed.

Manage your government correctly at the start of a war. 8
Close your borders and tear up passports.
Block the passage of envoys.
Encourage politicians at headquarters to stay out of it.
You must use any means to put an end to politics.
Your enemy's people will leave you an opening.
You must instantly invade through it.

[8]Immediately seize a place that they love.
Do it quickly.
Trample any border to pursue the enemy.
Use your judgment about when to fight.

[12]Doing the right thing at the start of war is like
approaching a woman.
Your enemy's men must open the door.
After that, you should act like a streaking rabbit.
The enemy will be unable to catch you.

♦ ♦ ♦

8 Warriors learn to manage those in authority over them.
You must control their access to outside information.
Control the channels of information.
Distance yourself from those concerned only with their own interests.
You must champion the shared goals of the organization.
Wait for a clear opportunity to act decisively.
Waste no time in taking advantage of that opportunity.

You must threaten your rivals' vulnerabilities.
Speed is the key.
Don't let imaginary barriers prevent you from challenging rivals.
Your training is the key to picking the right battles.

When you are in new, unfamiliar situations, you must be careful of other people's feelings.
Your opponents will eventually leave you an opening.
When you see that opening, use it immediately.
Put your rivals far behind you.

Chapter 12

Attacking with Fire: The Discipline of Danger

This chapter explains the danger of fire when it is used as a weapon. A fire attack is different from attacks from regular opponents. Fire leverages the larger forces in your environment. Warriors must always be aware of their situation so that they can be on guard against becoming a target for this particular form of attack. Though the chapter deals with the danger of fire specifically, it also teaches the discipline you must maintain in the face of any type of attack.

Your vigilance against danger starts by recognizing when you might become a target. Danger can not only threaten you personally; it can threaten your resources, friends, assets, and so on. Danger from the environment doesn't arise out of thin air. You should be able to easily spot the development of threatening conditions. These dangers take time to arise, and the best method for countering them is to remove yourself from dangerous situations long before they can hurt you.

When you are threatened by danger, your safety depends upon reacting correctly. The impersonal forces of the environment and society are dangerous on their own, but the danger is magnified if you panic. Panic leaves you open to more direct attacks by other opponents. You are always threatened by changes in the environment that your opponents can use against you.

In the end, the discipline to face dangers comes from your ability to control your emotions. In this sense, fire becomes a metaphor for the fire of rage, the most dangerous element of all.

Attacking with Fire

SUN TZU SAID:

There are five targets that can be attacked with fire. 1
The first targets for fire are troops.
The second targets for fire are supplies.
The third targets for fire are supply transports.
The fourth targets for fire are storehouses.
The fifth targets for fire are camps.

7To make fire, people must have the resources.
To build a fire, someone must prepare the raw materials.

9To attack with fire, it must be in the right season.
To start a fire, someone must take the time.

11One must select the right season.
The weather must be dry.

13One must select the right time.
The season is when the grass is as high as the side of a cart.

15You can tell the proper days by the stars in the night sky.
You want days when the wind rises in the morning.

The Discipline of Danger

THE WARRIOR HEARS:

1 Warriors are wary of leaving targets open to attack.
People can be targets.
Resources can be targets.
Channels of support can be targets.
Long-term assets can be targets.
Communities can be targets.

People cannot create the opportunity to target you.
Rivals can only use resources found in the environment.

The climate determines when you are vulnerable.
Enemies can work to use the environment against you.

Know when conditions are dangerous.
The fuel might exist all around you.

Know when others want to target you.
Realize that you might be sitting in a susceptible position.

Warriors know when climate changes are going against them.
They can feel the danger in the shifts in the wind.

Everyone attacks with fire. 2
People can create five different situations with fire and you
must be able to adjust to them.

³People can start a fire inside the enemy's camp.
Then they attack the enemy's periphery.

⁵People launch a fire attack, but the enemy remains calm.
They will then wait and not attack.

⁷The fire reaches its height.
Opponents will follow its path if they can.
If they can't follow it, they stay where they are.

¹⁰Spreading fires on the outside of camp can kill.
People can't always get fire inside the enemy's camp.
They take their time in spreading it.

¹³People set fire when the wind is at their back.
They won't attack into the wind.
Daytime winds last a long time.
Night winds fade quickly.

¹⁷Every army must know how to adjust to the five possible
attacks by fire.
Use many men to guard against them.

2 Warriors know that a threat can come from any direction. You must recognize the five different forms that environmental threats take and know how to counter them.

The leader of a group can have a problem.
Then enemies will attempt to pick off his supporters.

If you remain calm during crises, you are safe.
The real danger is when you panic.

Every crisis will reach a peak.
During these moments, avoid leaving your opponents an opening.
Without an opening, they cannot bring you down.

People can trigger little irritations all around you.
This is common when rivals cannot hurt you directly.
You must defend yourself for a long time.

You are in danger when things go against you.
When your luck changes, you are safe.
When your bad luck is well known, it can last a long time.
When no one knows about it, your luck can change quickly.

You can defend against any form of attack if you know what to expect.
All you need is vigilance.

People who use fire to assist their attacks are clever. 3
Water can add force to an attack.
People can also use water to disrupt an enemy.
It does not, however, take his resources.

You win in battle by getting the opportunity to attack. 4
It is dangerous if you fail to study how to accomplish this
achievement.
As commander, you cannot waste your opportunities.

4We say:
A wise leader plans success.
A good general studies it.
If there is little to be gained, don't act.
If there is little to win, do not use your men.
If there is no danger, don't fight.

10As leader, you cannot let your anger interfere with the suc-
cess of your forces.
As commander, you cannot let yourself become enraged
before you go to battle.
Join the battle only when it is in your advantage to act.
If there is no advantage in joining a battle, stay put.

14Anger can change back into happiness.
Rage can change back into joy.
A nation once destroyed cannot be brought back to life.
Dead men do not return to the living.

3 Warriors are wary of opponents who use the environment.
Changes in the environment can add ferocity to any attack.
Your progress is easy to stop if the climate is against you.
Forces in the environment can seriously damage you.

4 Warriors are always looking for paths to move forward.
You leave yourself open to attack when you fail to maintain the initiative.
You must grab opportunities when you see them.

Open your eyes.
You lead by virtue of your good judgment.
Others listen to you because they respect your knowledge.
The benefit of your actions must outweigh their cost.
Useless battles undermine everyone's support.
Avoid conflict unless it is more dangerous not to fight.

Warriors know how to control their emotions so that they can make good decisions.
Your decision to meet a challenge must be made with a clear head and a quiet heart.
You gain nothing by lashing out in anger.
If you have nothing to gain, you must hold your peace.

Emotions change like the weather.
Today's enemy can become tomorrow's friend.
When actions are destructive, you cannot take them back.
What you lose, you can lose forever.

[18]This fact must make a wise leader cautious.
A good general is on guard.

[20]Your philosophy must be to keep the nation peaceful and
the army intact.

♦ ♦ ♦

You must be sensitive about every action you choose.
You must also be sensitive to threats.

Your path to success depends on avoiding unnecessary conflict while you protect yourself.

Chapter 13

用 間

Using Spies: A Network of Sources

You have probably heard that success depends less on what you know than on who you know. In classical strategy, this idea is a little more sophisticated. Sun Tzu teaches that what you know depends on who you know. Information is the source of all strategy, but you can only get the most valuable information from having the right contacts. Strategy replaces force and effort with good information—which you obtain through cultivating the right sources.

The world is a dangerous place. Without the right information, you cannot properly prepare for its dangers. Most people spend too little time, effort, and money on getting good information. Warriors are different from ordinary people because they place a premium on staying informed. You must build and maintain a network of personal contacts if you want to be successful.

Information can be misleading, especially when it comes from only one type of source. Good strategy requires that warriors build a wide variety of contacts to provide a well-rounded view of every situation. Sun Tzu teaches specifically that five different types of sources are needed to create a complete view.

Developing and maintaining a good network of sources requires a special set of skills. Without the right social skills, you will never get the information you need. Without the information you need, you cannot develop a successful strategy. In many ways, Sun Tzu saves his most important lessons for the end of his book.

Using Spies

Sᴜɴ Tᴢᴜ sᴀɪᴅ:

All successful armies require thousands of men. 1
They invade and march thousands of miles.
Whole families are destroyed.
Other families must be heavily taxed.
Every day, a large amount of money must be spent.

6Internal and external events force people to move.
They are unable to work while on the road.
They are unable to find and hold a useful job.
This affects 70 percent of thousands of families.

10You can watch and guard for years.
Then a single battle can determine victory in a day.
Despite this, bureaucrats worship the value of their salary
money too dearly.
They remain ignorant of the enemy's condition.
The result is cruel.

15They are not leaders of men.
They are not servants of the state.
They are not masters of victory.

A Network of Sources

THE WARRIOR HEARS:

1 Warriors know their success depends upon many people.
Meeting challenges and going the distance don't assure success.
The risks are real.
Everyone makes sacrifices.
No matter how much you spend, you cannot buy your victories.

All people get pushed around by events beyond their control.
At some point, you will be forced to go job hunting.
You will go through periods when you cannot find work.
The competitive nature of the world makes nothing certain.

It can take years for the right opportunity to appear.
You must prepare for a decisive event that changes your life.
True success will never come from being a cog in the system and
saving your money.
Money is worthless if you remain ignorant of your opportunities.
You will miss out.

Without the right knowledge, you will always be a follower.
Without the right knowledge, you will never take the lead.
Without knowledge, you will never succeed.

¹⁸People need an intelligent leader and a worthy commander.
You must move your troops to the right places to beat others.
You must accomplish your attack and escape unharmed.
This requires foreknowledge.
You can obtain foreknowledge.
You can't get it from demons or spirits.
You can't see it from professional experience.
You can't check it with analysis.
You can only get it from other people.
You must always know the enemy's situation.

You must use five types of spies. 2
You need local spies.
You need inside spies.
You need double agents.
You need doomed spies.
You need surviving spies.

⁷You need all five types of spies.
No one must discover your methods.
You will then be able to put together a true picture.
This is the commander's most valuable resource.

¹¹You need local spies.
Get them by hiring people from the countryside.

¹³You need inside spies.
Win them by subverting government officials.

Others must see you as wise and skilled.

You must know enough to do the right thing at the right time.

You must know how to make progress in the face of danger.

You must know what others are thinking.

That information is available to you.

There is no magic in foreseeing the future.

You cannot trust in just your past experience.

Knowledge never comes from facts alone.

Only people can tell you what they are planning.

You must understand the positions others are in.

2 Warriors develop a variety of information channels.

You need information on your environment.

You need information on leaders.

You need information on your rivals.

You need to transmit misleading information.

You need timely information.

A single viewpoint is misleading.

People will tell you just what you want to hear.

You must overcome your preconceptions to see the truth.

You must protect your information sources and methods.

Some people know your battleground better than you do.

You must make contact with people with experience.

Insiders are close to decision-makers.

Only insiders know how those in authority think.

[15]You need double agents.
Discover enemy agents and convert them.

[17]You need doomed spies.
Deceive professionals into being captured.
Let them know your orders.
They will then take those orders to your enemy.

[21]You need surviving spies.
Someone must return with a report.

Your job is to build a complete army. 3
No relations are as intimate as the ones with spies.
No rewards are too generous for spies.
No work is as secret as that of spies.

[5]If you aren't clever and wise, you can't use spies.
If you aren't fair and just, you can't use spies.
If you can't see the small subtleties, you won't get the truth
from spies.

[8]Pay attention to small, trifling details!
Spies are helpful in every area.

[10]Spies are the first to hear information, so they must not
spread information.
Spies who give your location or talk to others must be
terminated along with those to whom they have talked.

Identify your rivals' information sources.
These people will allow you to understand your rivals' methods.

You must sacrifice some information channels.
The goal is to mislead others about your intentions.
You need to control people's perceptions.
Once you have misled a source, you cannot use him or her again.

Finally, there are sources you must protect.
You need critical news immediately.

3 Warriors seek out the whole story.
You must make your information sources into your best friends.
You must be willing to pay for good information.
You need to know what no one else knows.

You must learn what makes sense and what doesn't.
You must weigh each fact without prejudice.
You must especially pay attention to small details because details are difficult to fake.

The smallest minutiae give the truest picture.
Every scrap of information is important.

You must trust your sources to get you information quickly before its value disappears.
If your contacts give out confidential information about you, they do you more harm than good.

You may want to attack an army's position. 4
You may want to attack a certain fortification.
You may want to eliminate people in a certain place.
You must first know the guarding general.
You must know his left and right flanks.
You must know his hierarchy.
You must know the way in.
You must know where different people are stationed.
You must demand this information from your spies.

[10]You want to know the enemy spies in order to convert
them into your men.
You find sources of information and bribe them.
You must bring them in with you.
You must obtain them as double agents and use them as
your emissaries.

[14]Do this correctly and carefully.
You can contact both local and inside spies and obtain their
support.
Do this correctly and carefully.
You create doomed spies by deceiving professionals.
You can use them to give false information.
Do this correctly and carefully.
You must have surviving spies capable of bringing you infor-
mation at the right time.

4 Warriors need specific information to take specific actions.
Your ability to move forward always depends upon information.
Windows of opportunity open only at specific places and times.
When you know about powerful people, you know how to behave.
When you know about specific barriers, you can overcome them.
When you tackle a specific organization, you can outmaneuver it.
Your knowledge is the key that opens the door.
Your knowledge is the secret to avoiding conflict.
You must develop contacts to get this information.

The best place to start developing contacts is with people who are in
contact with your rivals.
They must find dealing with you rewarding.
You must befriend these people.
You can use these sources to get information from your opponents
and to misinform them.

Do not take chances with valuable sources.
You need to know people with special expertise and people who
know people with special expertise.
It takes work to build an information network.
You sometimes need to sacrifice an information source.
Providing misinformation can be extremely valuable.
You must pick the right situations.
You must protect key information sources because only they can get
you the most valuable news.

²¹These are the five different types of intelligence work.
You must be certain to master them all.
You must be certain to create double agents.
You cannot afford to be too cost conscious in creating these
double agents.

This technique created the success of ancient Shang. 5
This is how the Shang held their dynasty.

³You must always be careful of your success.
Learn from Lu Ya of Shang.

⁵Be a smart commander and a good general.
You do this by using your best and brightest people for spying.
This is how you achieve the greatest success.
This is how you meet the necessities of war.
The whole army's position and ability to move depends on
these spies.

✦ ✦ ✦

✦ ✦ ✦

You must suspect information that comes from only one source.
Act only on information that you can verify.
You must especially know your rivals' points of view.
Most people spend too little time and effort learning what their
rivals know.

5 Warriors throughout history have depended on information.
History's conquerors have been information magicians.

You can be as successful as any person in history.
All successful people use the same basic strategy.

You must make good decisions and provide dependable leadership.
Winning is much more a matter of information than of strength.
Information can help you achieve any goal you can imagine.
Success is a matter of consistently choosing the right challenges.
Your position in the world and your progress through life depend
on your network of sources.

Glossary of Key Concepts

The purpose of this glossary is to provide an overview of Sun Tzu's key strategic concepts. These Chinese characters are from *The Art of War Plus the Ancient Chinese Revealed,* and the concepts are discussed in depth in *The Art of War Plus Its Amazing Secrets.* We name the Chinese characters uniquely to make it easier to communicate these ideas. The Chinese terms shown are primarily Pinyin, but without the tone numbers. To eliminate confusing duplications, alternate Pinyin terms or Cantonese terms are also used to create unique names. These terms are not meant to represent any actual Chinese spoken dialect.

AI: 狹 *narrow, constricted*: a confined space or narrow niche; one of six field positions; the limited extreme of the dimension YUAN, distance; opposite of GUANG, wide.

BAO: 賞 *treasure, reward*: the necessary compensation for success; winning is not beating the competition, but producing a reward; victory must pay.

BEI: 北 *flee, northward*: run away without fighting; one of six weaknesses of an organization; opposite of JEUN, advance.

BENG: 崩 *split apart, collapse*: fall apart over time; one of six weaknesses of an organization.

BI: 避 *evade, avoid*: the strategy used by small competitors when facing large opponents.

BIAN: 變 *change, transform*: transition from one condition to another; the ability to adapt to different situations.

BING: 兵 *weapons, soldiers, war*: competition; the use of force.

BU: 不 *no, not*: negates the meaning of the following ideogram; the character that provides the opposing idea for concepts that have no natural opposite.

BU ZHI: 不知 *not to know, ignorance*: a failure to understand or to gather information; the cardinal sin in BING-FA; opposite of ZHI, knowledge.

CHENG: 城 *city*: fortified town; populated position that is costly to attack.

CHI: 治 *govern, rule, control*: literally, to harness a river; to manage or govern people or situations; the opposite of JUAN, disorder.

CHING: 情 *feelings, affection, love, situation*: the bonds of relationship that must be managed like other situations.

CHONG: 重 *serious, heavy*: requiring effort and skill; the situation of being deeply committed to a campaign, with opposition behind; one of nine situations or types of terrain.

CONG: 從 *follow*: to obey, to submit to, and to trail; opposite of GWO, pass.

CU: 趣 *hurry*: to rush into or to be attracted to; a dangerous method to move; opposite of DAI, wait.

DA: 大 *big, large*: forces that are much larger than opponents' forces; opposite of SIU, small.

DAI: 待 *wait, await*: staying in place patiently; nonaction when there is no opportunity; the opposite of CU, hurry.

DI: 地 *ground, earth, situation, condition*: a specific place, condition, or situation; where one competes and simultaneously the prize of competition; one of five key factors in competitive analysis; opposite of TIAN, heaven.

DIE: 至 *arrive, reach, stop*: end of movement to a destination or goal; opposite of HEUI, to go.

DIK: 敵 *enemy, opponent*: someone who desires the same position; a competitor.

DUI: 隊 *group, team, troop*: a grouping of people; one of the five targets of fire attacks.

DUN: 鈍 *blunt, dull*: a slow mental attitude; opposite of RIU, sharp.

FA: 法 *method, laws*: procedures, techniques; steps to accomplish a goal; one of the five key factors in analysis; the realm of groups that must follow procedures; the conceptual opposite of JIANG, the general, who is free from law because he makes the law.

FAN: 反 *reverse, flip, double back, double agent*: to turn around in direction; to change a situation; to switch a person's alligiance; one of five types of spies.

FEI: 費 *waste, waste time, consume*: to expend limited resources; the result of unnecessary conflict.

FEN: 分 *divide, separate*: to break apart a larger force; opposite of HAP, to join, and ZHUAN, to concentrate.

FENG: 風 *wind, custom, fashion*: the pressure of environmental forces; a necessary ingredient for fire or environment attacks.

GAAN: 間 *spies, conduits*: literally, openings between things; go-betweens, channels of information.

GAI: 計 *plan, planning*: analysis of a situation; used as a combination of ZHI (knowledge) and JAIN (vision); used in combination with GUI (deception) to create GUI GAI, deceptive plans, tricks, or traps.

GONG: 攻 *attack, strike*: any action against an opponent; a movement into new territory; the opposite of SHOU, to defend.

GONG CHENG: 攻城 *siege, strike city*: any action against an entrenched position; one of the five basic attacks; the least desirable form of attack.

GUA: 懸 *hanging, suspended, entangling*: a position that cannot be returned to; any condition that leaves no place to go; one of six field positions.

GUANG: 廣 *wide*: lacking constraint; ground form opposite of AI, narrow.

GUI: 詭 *illusion, deception*: misleading the competition; an attack on an opponent's JAIN, vision; the essence of war.

GUO: 國 *nation*: state; the productive part of an organization; the seat of political power; the entity that controls an army or competitive part of the organization.

GWAI: 貴 *expensive*: costly in terms of money or resources; closely related conceptually to the idea of FEI, to consume or waste.

GWO: 過 *pass, pass through, go across*: to exceed or surpass; opposite of CONG, follow.

HAAM: 陷 *sink, plunge, trap*: fall down or into; one of six weaknesses of organizations.

HANG: 行 *act, march, go, walk*: action toward a position or goal; used as a near synonym for DONG, act.

HAP: 合 *join*: to unite with allies to create a larger force; opposite of FEN, divide.

HEI: 氣 *spirit, air, steam, gas*: something insubstantial; a characteristic of DONG, movement so opponents cannot know a position.

HEUI: 去 *go away*: to depart; to leave an area; opposite of DIE, arrive.

HUO: 火 *fire*: the only weapon whose use Sun Tzu details; used as an analogy for attacks in general and environmental attacks in particular.

JANG: 正 *straight, right, proper, correct*: the expected normal behavior; the standard approach; the opposite of QI, unusual.

JEUN: 進 *advance, make progress*: to move forward in a campaign; opposite of BEI, retreat.

JI: 糧 *savings, stores, accumulate*: resources that have been stored up; one of the five targets of fire attacks.

JIANG: 將 *general, commander*: the leader of an army; the decision-maker in a competitive unit; the superior of officers and men; one of the five key factors in analysis; the conceptual opposite of FA, the laws that do not require decisions.

JIAO: 來 *meeting, joining, crossing*: to come together; to intersect; an open situation that encourages a race; one of nine situations or types of terrain.

JIE: 節 *restraint, to restrain*: to withhold action until the proper time; a companion concept to SHI, momentum.

JIK: 直 *direct, straight*: a straight or obvious path to a goal; opposite of YU, detour.

JING: 政 *government, political affairs*: the force of authority, the ability to organize.

JIU: 九 *nine, many*: used to indicate many different types as well as the specific number.

JIU: 久 *long time, delay*: avoiding action for a period of time; lacking immediacy.

JUAN: 亂 *chaos, disorder*: conditions that cannot be predicted exactly; the natural state of confusion arising from competition; one of six weaknesses of an organization; opposite of CHI, control.

JUN: 軍 *army, armed*: pertaining to a military force; the most dangerous type of ZHENG, conflict.

KE: 客 *guest, invader*: inside an opponent's territory; one who consumes resources.

KEUI: 驅 *drive, expel*: to motivate people to move and to keep them moving.

KU: 庫 *houses, storehouses*: places where supplies can be stockpiled; one of the five targets for fire attacks.

LEI: 力 *force*: power in the simplest sense; with dominant energy.

LI: 利 *advantage, benefit*: an opportunity arising from having a better position relative to opponents; a key characteristic of position.

LIANG: 糧 *provisions, resources, food*: necessary supplies, most commonly food; one of the five targets of fire attacks.

LING: 令 *command*: orders or the act of ordering subordinates.

LIU: 陸 *plateau, land, continent*: one of the five types of land; analogy for level, solid, and certain ground.

LU: 奪 *seize*: to catch; to capture; to imprison; to take control of desired ground to discourage an opponent's attack.

LUE: 掠 *, plunder, rob, take by force*: gathering provisions from enemy territory.

NEI: 內 *inside, internal*: within a territory or organization; an insider; one of five types of spies; opposite of WAI, external.

PI: 圯 *ruined, bad*: destroyed; terrain that is broken and difficult to traverse; one of the nine situations or types of terrain.

PO: 破 *broken, divide*: an attack on QUAN, whole, and the opposite of YI, oneness.

QI: 奇 *strange, unusual, odd, improper, surprise*: the unexpected; the surprising; the result of the creative impulse; the opposite of JANG, straight.

QI JANG: 奇 正 *innovation*: a combination of QI, the unusual, and JANG, the standard; the change that creates SHI, momentum.

QING: 輕 *easy, light*: requiring little effort; a situation that requires little effort; one of nine situations or types of terrain; opposite of CHONG, dangerous or serious.

QU: 衢 *highway, intersecting*: a situation or type of ground that facilitates travel; one of nine types of terrain.

QUAN: 全 *complete, whole*: the sense of lacking nothing needed or being finished; creates YI, oneness or unity; arises from TAO, philosophy; the opposite of PO, divided.

REN: 人 *man, men, person, people*: members of an army or organization; individuals; one of the five targets of fire attacks.

RIU: 銳 *sharp, keen*: acuity of mind; the fine point of a weapon; opposite of DUN, dull.

SAN: 散 *scatter, scattering*: to disperse; a situation that causes a force to scatter; one of nine conditions or types of terrain.

SAT: 壹 *full, substantial, wealthy, strong*: the state of being crowded; the opposite of XU, empty.

SHAANG: 生 *birth, born*: creation; one of five types of spies; opposite of SI, dead.

SHAN: 善 *good, virtuous*: acting correctly; making the correct decisions.

SHAN: 山 *mountain, hill, peak*: one of four types of land; analogy for uneven places with peaks and valleys.

SHANG: 上 *above, up, before, better than*: superiority in time or position; opposite of XIA, below.

SHAO: 寡 *few*: a small force or group; a weak point exhibiting the characteristic of XU, emptiness; opposite of ZHONG, crowd.

SHEN: 神 *spirit, ghost, supernatural being*: the essence of a person or group of people.

SHI: 勢 *influence, force, momentum*: used specifically by Sun Tzu as the result of QI JANG, innovation; in some ways the opposite of JIE, restraint.

SHII: 弛 *relax, loosen*: too lax; too easygoing; one of six weaknesses of an army.

SHOU: 守 *defend, defense*: to guard or keep a possession; to remain in a position; the opposite of GONG, attack.

SHU: 數 *count, calculate, number*: mathematical evaluation of a situation.

SHUI: 水 *water, fluid*: one of four types of land; analogy for fluid conditions that change rapidly.

SI: 死 *death, dead, deadly, extreme*: termination of life or efforts; an extreme situation in which the only option is to fight; one of nine situations or types of terrain; one of five types of spies; opposite of SAANG, birth.

SING: 勝 *victory, to win*: success in an endeavor; winning a battle; the only goal of BING-FA; it produces more than it consumes.

SIU: 少 *little, small*: forces that are small in relative size; the opposite of DA, big.

SOU: 走 *misstep, go astray*: used to describe being outmaneuvered; one of six weaknesses of an army.

SUO: 所 *place, location*: a specific position on the ground, common term to indicate a position.

TAO: 道 *philosophy, way*: a system of thought; literally "road" or "path," as in the "path to victory"; one of five key factors in analysis.

TIAN: 天 *heaven*: divine providence; climate; weather; trends that change over time; one of five key factors in analysis.

TING: 聽 *listen, understand, obey*: to gather knowledge, ZHI.

TONG: 通 *open, unobstructed, expert*: without obstacles or barriers; available for easy movement; accepting of new ideas; one of six field positions; opposite of XIAN, obstructed.

WAI: 外 *external, outside*: not within a territory or organization; an outsider; a remote perspective that gives an objective view; opposite of NEI, internal.

WAN: 萬 *myriad*: a large, complex group; a big organization.

WEI: 圍 *surround, confined*: to encircle; the normal tactic for a much larger force encapsulating a smaller one; the characteristic of a special transitional situation in which a larger force can be attacked by a smaller one; one of nine situations or types of terrain.

WU: 吳 *boast, an ancient Chinese kingdom*: name of the kingdom for which Sun Tzu was hired as a general.

XIA: 下 *below, under, following*: a lower position or status; opposite of SHANG, above.

XIAN: 險 *obstacles, obstructed*: containing obstacles; one of six field positions; opposite of TONG, unobstructed.

XIANG: 鄉 *countryside, local*: having local knowledge; knowing a specific ground; one of five types of spies.

XIAO: 效 *learn, compare, proofread:* to compare qualities between two competing opponents; to double-check.

XIN: 心 *feeling, emotion*: a visceral reaction to JIAN, vision, necessary to inspire DONG, action; an important component of esprit de corps; never a sufficient cause for GONG, attack.

XING: 形 *form, position*: a shape or condition of DI, the ground; using the benefits of the ground; formations of troops; bringing together resources at a specific time and place; one of four key skills in making progress.

XU: 處 *emptiness, insubstantial, weakness*: devoid of force; identifying a point of attack or a path of movement; full of need; needy, poor; the opposite of SAT, full.

YANG: 陽 *south, sunny hillside, male principle*: used to mean a strong position; opposite of YIN, north, shady hillside.

YAO: 事 *profession, business, affair, to serve*: a thing that needs to be done; skill; ability; responsibility.

YI: 一 *one, oneness*: the first number, used by Sun Tzu to indicate unity; opposite of ZHONG, crowd, in one sense, and PO, divided, in another.

YIN: 陰 *north, shady hillside, the female principle*: used to mean a weak position; opposite of YANG, south, sunny hillside.

YONG: 勇 *brave, bravery*: courage of conviction; willingness to act on vision; one of six characteristics of a leader.

YOU: 誘 *entice:* to lure an opponent away from a position; a method of GUI, deception.

YU: 迂 *detour*: the indirect or unsuspected path to a goal; the more difficult path to opportunity; opposite of JIK, direct.

YUAN: 遠 *distance, far, spread-out*: remote from current location; occupying positions that are not close to one another; one of six field positions; one of three dimensions for evaluating opportunities; the most extreme case of this dimension.

YUE: 曰 *say, called*: to talk, to discuss; used to identify key concepts that require discussion in the original Chinese.

YUN: 均 *equal, fair*: evenly balanced situation; lack of advantage or disadvantage.

ZE: 澤 *marsh, swamp*: one of four types of land; analogy for uncertain situations.

ZHAN: 戰 *battle*: meeting an opponent or challenge; literally "one weapon"; not necessarily fighting, as in the idea of conflict, ZHENG.

ZHENG: 爭 *conflict, contentious, disputed*: direct confrontation of arms; the nature of highly desirable ground; one of nine types of DI, terrain or situations.

ZHI: 知 *know, knowledge*: to understand or comprehend; the basis of all other skills; the foundation of success.

ZHII: 支 *support, supporting*: to prop up; to enhance; one of six field positions; the opposite extreme of GUA, entangling.

ZHUAN: 專 *concentrate, focus*: the process of bringing resources together for a single purpose; the opposite of FEN, divide.

ZI: 輜 *supply wagons*: the transportation of supplies; one of five targets of fire attacks.

ZONG: 眾 *crowd*: large group of people; a strong concentration of forces at a certain position; the opposite of SHOA, few.

About the Translator and Author

Gary Gagliardi is recognized as America's leading expert on Sun Tzu's *The Art of War*. An award-winning author and businessperson, he is known for his ability to put sophisticated concepts into simple, easy-to-understand terms. He appears on hundreds of talk shows nationwide, providing strategic insight on the breaking news.

Gary began studying the Chinese classic more than thirty years ago, applying its principles first to his own career, then to building a successful business, and finally in training the world's largest organizations to be more competitive. He has spoken all over the world on a variety of topics concerning competition, from modern technology to ancient history. His books have been translated into many languages, including Japanese, Korean, Russian, and Spanish.

Gary began using Sun Tzu's competitive principles in a successful corporate career but soon started his own software company. In 1990, he wrote his first *Art of War* adaptation for his company's salespeople. By 1992, his company was on *Inc.* magazine's list of the 500 fastest-growing privately held companies in America. After Gary won the U.S. Chamber of Commerce **Blue Chip Quality Award** and became an Ernst and Young **Entrepreneur of the Year** finalist, his customers— AT&T, GE, and Motorola, among others—began inviting him to speak at their conferences. Jardin's, the original Hong Kong trading company known as "The Noble House," became one of his partners and even gave him the honor of firing the noontime cannon in Hong Kong's harbor. After becoming a multimillionaire when he sold his software company in 1997, he continued teaching *The Art of War* around the world.

Gary has authored several breakthrough works on *The Art of War*. In 1999, he translated each Chinese character to demonstrate the equation-like symmetry of Sun Tzu's work. In 2003, his work *The Art of War Plus The Ancient Chinese Revealed* won the **Independent Publishers Book Award** as the year's best new multicultural nonfiction work. In 2004, his adaptation of Sun Tzu's principles to marketing, *The Art of War Plus The Art of Marketing*, was selected as one of the year's three best business books by the **Ben Franklin Book Awards committee**. In 2004, he released a new work that explains the many hidden aspects of Sun Tzu's text, *The Art of War Plus Its Amazing Secrets*, which was selected as a **Highlighted Title** by Independent Publishers.

Gary has also written a large number of other adaptations of *The Art of War*, applying Sun Tzu's methods to areas such as career building, management, small business, and even romance and parenting. Gary lives near Seattle with his wife.

Art of War Gift Books

Mastering Strategy Series

^{Sun Tzu's} The Art of War Plus The Warrior's Apprentice
A first book on strategy for the novice.

^{Sun Tzu's} The Art of War Plus The Ancient Chinese Revealed
See the original! Each original Chinese character individually translated.

^{Sun Tzu's} The Art of War Plus Its Amazing Secrets
Learn the hidden secrets! The deeper meaning of Sun Tzu explained.

The Warrior Class: 306 Lessons in Strategy
The complete study guide! Simple lessons in strategy you can read any time.

Career and Business Series

^{Sun Tzu's} The Art of War Plus The Art of Career Building
For everyone! Use Sun Tzu's lessons to advance your career.

^{Sun Tzu's} The Art of War Plus The Art of Sales
For salespeople! Use Sun Tzu's lessons to win sales and keep customers.

^{Sun Tzu's} The Art of War Plus The Art of Management
For managers! Use Sun Tzu's lessons on managing teams more effectively.

^{Sun Tzu's} The Art of War Plus Strategy for Sales Managers
For sales managers! Use Sun Tzu's lessons to direct salespeople more effectively.

^{Sun Tzu's} The Art of War Plus The Art of Small Business
For business owners! Use Sun Tzu's lessons in building your own business.

^{Sun Tzu's} The Art of War Plus The Art of Marketing
For marketing professionals! Use Sun Tzu's lessons to win marketing warfare.

Life Strategies Series

^{Sun Tzu's} The Art of War Plus The Art of Love
For lifelong love! *Bing-fa* applied to finding, winning, and keeping love alive.

^{Sun Tzu's} The Art of War Plus The Art of Parenting Teens
For every parent! Strategy applied to protecting, guiding, and motivating teens.

Current Events Series

^{Sun Tzu's} The Art of War Plus Strategy against Terror
An examination of the War on Terror using Sun Tzu's timeless principles.

Audio and Video

Amazing Secrets of *The Art of War*: Audio
1 1/2 Hours 2-CD set

Amazing Secrets of *The Art of War*: Video
1 1/2 Hours VHS

To Order On-line: Visit www.BooksOnStrategy.com
Fax Orders: 206-546-9756. Voice: 206-533-9357.